CONFESSIONS

OF A SMALL PRESS

RACKETEER

CONFESSIONS OF A SMALL PRESS RACKETEER

Stuart Ross

ANVIL PRESS | VANCOUVER

Confessions of a Small Press Racketeer
Copyright © 2005 by Stuart Ross

NATIONAL LIBRARY OF CANADA CATALOGUING IN PUBLICATION DATA
Ross, Stuart
    Confessions of a small press racketeer / Stuart Ross.
ISBN: 1-895636-65-5

1. Ross, Stuart.   2. Authors, Canadian (English) — 20th century — Biography.
3. Editors — Canada — Biography.   4. Small presses — Canada.
I. Title.
PS8585.O841Z463 2005   C818'.5409   C2005-901901-8

Printed and bound in Canada
Cover design: Rayola Graphic Design
Typesetting: HeimatHouse

Represented in Canada by the Literary Press Group
Distributed by the University of Toronto Press

The publisher gratefully acknowledges the financial assistance of the B.C. Arts Council, the Canada Council for the Arts, and the Book Publishing Industry Development Program (BPIDP) for their support of our publishing program.

Anvil Press
P.O. Box 3008, Main Post Office
Vancouver, B.C. V6B 3X5   CANADA
www.anvilpress.com

"They'd pick it up, and they'd see there are three words to a page, and kind of flip, flip, flip, and they'd be through it in thirty seconds and say, 'What the fuck was that?' and slam it down on the shelf. So I knew I was up against, as they say in the trade, consumer resistance."
— bpNichol, in conversation with Stuart Ross
in *Mondo Hunkamooga*, October 1983

In memory of bpNichol, 1944-1988

and for all the folders, staplers, rubber-stampers, and stitchers
who preceded him, accompanied him,
and follow in his wake

CONTENTS

INTRODUCTION

I DON'T KNOW what it is exactly that draws some people to the obsessive little universe of literary small press publishing, but I suspect it's the same thing that makes others join protest marches, spray-paint graffiti on the marble walls of banks, and canvass for a progressive political candidate who has no chance of winning the riding. That is to say, small press is radical, idealistic, and a *great* way to lose money.

Some writers use the small presses as a stepping stone to more commercial careers, and some people run their small presses only until they have families to feed and other adult responsibilities. Or until they realize there's neither fame nor fortune involved. Others are lifers: the Canadian poet bpNichol, the American Larry Fagin, the Brit Bob Cobbing. For them, as both writers and publishers, the small press is (in the case of Fagin) and was (in the cases of the late Nichol and Cobbing) an integral part of the fluid experiment of poetry and fiction. Perhaps it's also a way of life.

Toronto poet Victor Coleman, another lifer, and a founder of the legendary Coach House Press, likes to differentiate between the micropress and the small press. I imagine the distinction goes something like this: a micropress is a one-person operation doing very small print runs and paying costs out of pocket, while the small press — which falls somewhere between a micropress and a trade house — is a larger entity with a staff, a fall catalogue, perhaps an office, and, likely, some government funding. Although I occasionally employ Victor's terms, I consider both creatures small presses. They're both committed to publishing out-of-the-mainstream literature, and they both place this commitment above being profitable. You can call them whatever you want.

I started up my own small press, Proper Tales, when I was 20, back in 1979. I had no idea where this adventure would ultimately take me, but now, 26 years later, it's clear that it's defined my life — at least, my life as a writer, and as a reader of poetry and fiction. While it's true that — like the big presses — the small presses produce grotesque amounts of crap, they've also coughed up much of the most exciting and pleasurable works, and certainly the most innovative. Great things can happen when "business" and "profit" step aside. Whatever capitalism is good for — and I haven't figured that one out yet — it certainly isn't good for art.

In mid-2001, Shelagh Rowan-Legg, at that time the editor of the free monthly tabloid *Word: Toronto's Literary Calendar,* asked me if I'd like a column in the mag. I could write about anything I wanted. I liked this idea of having a regular place to vent and told her I'd write about the small press world, and my life in it as a writer and publisher. We settled on a bimonthly schedule, so it wouldn't become a grind. I would call it "Hunkamooga," a reference to my defunct zine about the small press scene, *Mondo Hunkamooga.*

As my first column, "I Am the King of Poetry," appeared in September 2001, Shelagh decided to step down from the mag. Maria Erskine, a secret writer of poems and a familiar face around the small press scene, took over as editor, and I had a new boss. And so, every two months since then, Maria has gently prodded me as I consistently missed deadline by a few hours or a few days.

Confessions of a Small Press Racketeer collects all the "Hunkamooga" columns published between September 2001 and February 2005, plus four new ones, written mainly in January 2005. The date after each column refers to the date of publication; the columns were written the month before. I've also added postscripts to many of the columns, to catch you up on new developments, lessons learned, and random afterthoughts. Most of these columns were written — after a few days' mulling — in an hour or two, while I spent a leisurely month or so preparing this manuscript for Anvil. I've edited and expanded some of the pieces, adding material I might have included at the time of writing if not for the 750-word limit (which Maria sometimes let balloon to 900). An abandoned column from June 2004 was turned into "Sometimes I Feel Like a Childless Writer, or Regrets, I've Had, Uh, Two," and another, from October 2003, was integrated into "The Comfort of Misery."

I keep threatening to quit my gig with *Word*, and I occasionally dream of taking the column somewhere that might actually pay. But I never do it. The truth is — and perhaps this is the key to the small press world — there's freedom in doing things for free.

*   *   *

Some expressions of gratitude are in order. For feedback and support, I'd like to thank Dana Samuel, who doesn't *have* to read the stuff, after all, and Maria Erskine, who does. Also, Alana Wilcox, Kevin Connolly, Gary Barwin, Elyse Friedman, Mako Funasaka, Joe Grengs, and Mary Jankulak.

And then there's Shelagh Rowan-Legg; *Word*'s former publisher, Mike O'Connor; *Word*'s current publisher, Bev Daurio; Robert Lecker, who bugged me to tackle the personal essay; and those who have run the Toronto Small Press Book Fair. Thanks also to the citizens of Ontario through the Ontario Arts Council's excellent Writer's Reserve Programme. And to Brian Kaufman and Jenn Farrell of Anvil Press, for their care and enthusiasm.

Stuart Ross
Toronto, February 2005

I AM THE KING OF POETRY

I AM THE king of the poetry kingdom. I decide everything. I will make or break you. You will not write a haiku unless I give the thumbs-up. You will apply to me for a licence to insert slant rhymes in your doggerel. Please enclose $25 with the application. The sooner I process it, the sooner you can enjoy a little slice of the poetry-fame pie. I run every series, edit every anthology, and sit on every jury. Agents pant at my ankles and wait for me to snap my fingers.

It's been tough. I mean, all of that while mentoring pretty much every young poet in town. And the older ones, too — they dodder and forget, and they really have no perspective on their own work anymore. They need a younger mentor. I let them know when to slip a Buffalo Tom reference into their poems. Or an Arthur Lyman reference, which is ironic, because he's from *their* time.

I'm really exhausted, as you can imagine. It's been difficult finding time for my own writing. And the country is starving for it. But I didn't choose to wear the poetry crown. It's just that I'm the only one whose head it fits. They came to me with it, and begged me to try it on, that crown. And I know that if I don't wear it, it'll perch on the noggin of someone whose head is either too big or too small. My head is just the right size. I didn't ask for the right-sized head, though.

Geez, I just stopped for a moment and rifled through my pockets. They're bulging with ideas. Found a few scraps with lines written on them that I don't want anymore. You can have them, and you don't even need to acknowledge me. I know that you appreciate me. I know where we stand. I know that I am your greatest influence. Here, take any of these, but put only as much on your plate as you can eat:

Spherical cantaloupe,
you perfect breast
with a price sticker on you.
*

I suffocated the kitten
because it saw into my soul.
*

Like the master chef with his frying pan,
he rustles up words that scan.
*

And then they'll come for the poets.

So, like I said, they're all yours. Poetry is about generosity. It is about sharing our language, our thoughts, our ideas. Poetry is what my eyes tell your eyes and what your eyes tell my eyes, and our eyes can pickpocket each other's sockets (perhaps making of them "picksockets," if you'll indulge me — which you better, or your career is finished), because ideas and images and beauty — yes, beauty — cannot be copyrighted. I propose that we do not sign our poems in the future, because does it truly matter who writes what? A poem is a poem, and inherently it belongs to the world, the earth, the people.

Or, better yet, I can simply be the Poetry Everyman, and we can all sign *my* name to our poems. It doesn't matter to me. Besides, I'm so busy making all your careers that I barely have time to write my own stuff.

Imagine this: you walk into a bookstore and you go to the poetry section. Of course, in this wondrous dreamworld, the poetry section is right at the front, by the cash register, and you must elbow the teeming others out of the way to even get a peek at the shelves. And when you do, you see that alphabetization has been a cinch — everything is under "R". Under "Ross". Where it should be. All poetry has been gathered under one populist umbrella. It's like Cuba, where you can cast your vote only for Fidel. And, as Castro says, this is the greater expression of democracy, this one-party system. After all, the multi-party system divides people. Does not the multi-poet system also divide people?

Let us all come together under my name. I shall bring unity. Let the cliques crumble. Let the petty back-stabbing come to an end. Let me fill every space in the interminable open mics. Send to me every poetry groupie, male or female. Yes, I am reluctant, but I will do as you say — I will take up the mantle this groundswell foists rudely upon me. My back is not strong, but I will carry the burden. I am tired, but I will not sleep. Sprinkle nails and tacks upon my mattress.

You pay for the pizza; I'll look after poetry.

September 2001

"AND BECAUSE IT IS MY HEART"

A PACKAGE COMES to my door. It's a bundle of seven self-published chapbooks by the brilliant American poet Bill Knott. In huge type at the beginning of each non-descript book: "It should be obvious that if I could have found a real publisher for this book, I wouldn't be doing it myself; no-one wants the humiliation of being a vanity author." Some of the books even feature lists of publishers and editors that have rejected his work.

Now, Knott is pretty big stuff in the States. At least, he was in the 1960s through the early '90s, before poetry there was ruled by wankers like Jorie Graham. Knott has books out from U of Iowa, Random House, Sun, Boa Editions (he calls them "the snakes from Boa Constrictor Press"). And now, it seems, no one will publish him to his satisfaction. He's fucking bitter.

Yeah, and me too. I mean, I just had my third spiney book of poetry published by ECW Press (*Razovsky at Peace* — buy it!), and I'm happy as a clam about that, but I've been at this racket since I was 15 (I'm 42 now), so I've got a lot to be bitter about.

Here's a little inventory of bitterness about my literary career. You might enjoy it over tea and crumpets:

• I got one stinkin' Works in Progress grant from the Ontario Arts Council in 1993, freeing me from indentured servitude at Harlequin Books, but nothing since. Meanwhile, all these peers and sub-peers and people like Dennis Bock with huge advances are snorting up the grant money with their jury-pleasing purple prose.

• *This Magazine* keeps making everyone but me their literary editor.

• I'm getting old! I know I'm not what I used to hate as a teenage writer, but I *look* like I am!

• No press has asked me to be their poetry editor, even though I know who all the good poets are who don't have books from big literary presses. (Well, Beth Follett at Pedlar asked me to edit Alice Burdick's first stunning per-fect-bound book, which is great, but who's gonna finally let me put a Daniel f. Bradley or Mark Laba book through the press? I mean, haven't we seen enough books for a while by Bruce Whiteman and rob mclennan and A.F. Moritz and Adeena Karasick?)

• Way crappier writers than me get more attention, because they're so god-damn self-absorbed and have no problem with their overinflated egos.

• My dad died before *Razovsky at Peace* came out, even though I got ECW to move it ahead a season. And my mom didn't live to see *any* of my swanky books published. Well, maybe I'm just sad about that, not bitter.

• Nick Power and I started the Toronto Small Press Book Fair — the first fair of its kind in Canada — and people don't genuflect before us wher-ever we go. Bow, you fuckers!

• The amazing Ottawa International Writers Festival is the only such fes-tival to invite me to read, even though I'm a better reader than nearly everyone else, and I never go into overtime.

• Hey, my second book of poetry — *Farmer Gloomy's New Hybrid* — was one of only seven titles shortlisted for the 2000 Trillium Book Award, given to the best book in any genre published in Ontario, but it didn't get reviewed anywhere of record.

• Open-mic sets are the blight of the literary world. That's not bitterness, but I really wanted to mention it. It's dreadful enough to be a "featured" writer for $25, but to have to sit through all that crap before I read . . . (And half those open-setters leave immediately after they've done their five minutes about their cat and their grandmother and their loneliness. They don't care about anyone else's poetry.)

• I was checking out the poetry section of a Chapters bookstore in London, Ontario, and found recent books by Ken Babstock, Paul Vermeersch, George Murray, and David McGimpsey, but nothing by me. Is it that they don't stock surrealists or they don't stock Jews? Chapters sucks, anyway — I'm also bitter because I should never have walked through their doors.

Stephen Crane, my favourite poet when I was a teenager, wrote:

In the desert
I saw a creature, naked, bestial,
who, squatting upon the ground,
Held his heart in his hands,
And ate of it.
I said, "Is it good, friend?"
"It is bitter — bitter," he answered;
"But I like it
Because it is bitter,
And because it is my heart."

18

Translated, that means, send Bill Knott a pile of U.S. money at WLP Dept., Emerson College, 100 Beacon St., Boston, Mass., 02116, and get some of his books. He's a lot better than Michael Ondaatje.

November 2001

In early 2003, I got my hands on a copy of Bill Knott's second book, Auto-necrophilia *(Big Table, 1971). It was stranger and more spectacular than I could have imagined and I was saddened that it was so long out of print. I wrote Knott and proposed that I do a reprint in chapbook form. I figured I could make a better-looking chapbook than he was capable of, and I could get a couple hundred copies into the hands of Canadians. In a series of brief curmudgeonly notes, he ascertained that I was serious, and suggested instead that I publish a collection of more recent poems. He sent me a crazy, complex, fabulous manuscript called* Lessons from the Orphanage and Other Poems, *and it sunk in that I was actually going to publish a book by* Bill Knott! *Which I did, a few months later. Since then, Knott's star has risen yet again, as Farrar Straus Giroux, John Ashbery's publisher, decided to follow the Proper Tales Press example and put out Knott's* The Unsubscriber, *in hardcover, in fall 2004. You better buy it or I'll kick your ass. Funny thing is, shortly after* The Unsubscriber's *publication, Knott released another flurry of self-published chapbooks, these ones with their titles scrawled in crayon on the covers. He's amazing!*

There was also some immediate fallout from this column. Bev Daurio approached me at the now-defunct Idler Pub (where Stan Rogal ran a weekly reading series for a decade, the fool). She had read my inventory of bitterness, and was willing to let me publish a poetry book of my choice through her Mercury Press. Visions of Mark Laba's first perfect-bound collection danced through my skull. I mean, that was the book I'd always dreamed of. Getting a manuscript out of Mark proved a difficult task — he was all enthusiasm, but just couldn't cough up the goods. I was in Toronto, and he was in Vancouver, so it wasn't like I could just drop by and rifle through his poems. Finally, I spelled out my terms: if the book was going to happen, then Clint Burnham, a mutual pal who also lives in Vancouver, was coming over to his place that weekend, and Mark had to give him access to all his papers. Clint would gather everything he could, send it to me, and I'd construct the new book from it. The threat was effective: when Clint arrived that weekend, Mark handed him a haphazard manuscript that would eventually become Dummy Spit. Dummy Spit is unlike any Canadian poetry book ever published before. It is part stand-up Yiddish vaudeville, part surrealist tour-de-force, and part poetic B-movie. It's mad genius. I'm sure it's sold at least nine copies.

Oh yeah, and a few years later I became the Literary Editor for This Magazine, got invited to another literary festival or two, and scored another few grants, one of which allowed me to quit (in disgust) my job at the corporate monstrosity that is eye Weekly. But I've thought up all sorts of new stuff to be bitter about!

LIVE POETS, IN THE RAIN

ONE RAINY NIGHT in October, while Canada was at war, I decided to take in a couple of readings.

At the Annette Public Library, out in Toronto's west-end Junction neighbourhood, Lillian Necakov was giving her first reading in years. I descended into the library's basement, into a brightly lit little room. A metre-high heap of plastic children's toys leaned against one wall. The audience of 11 — a couple of local writers, a couple of innocent library patrons, Lil's brother Eli, a few of her friends and library co-workers — sat in a semi-circle of chairs facing the chair Lillian would sit in. At the moment, she was passing a paper plate of cookies around. Giving out cookies at your reading is not hip, but the cookies were pretty good.

Lillian's the author of the poetry collections *Polaroids* (Coach House Books), *A Sickbed of Dogs* (Wolsak & Wynn), and *Hat Trick* (Exile Editions), as well as a bunch of chapbooks from a variety of presses, including her own Surrealist Poets' Gardening Assoc. She's a busy-as-hell working mom of two, and doesn't have much time to make the literary scene. Last time the West was on a bombing spree, it was her childhood home of Belgrade that ended up smouldering.

Anyway, she said hi to us, thanked us for coming, took her seat, and read a few selections from her books, but mainly from new work, a series of sprawling, image-laden, visceral poems. In fact, one — addressed to the dead child of a friend — was so moving that it had the whole audience nearly in tears. And Lillian herself wept during the last couple of lines. Yeah, I know it sounds sappy, but this was serious, important work about loss — and it was strange, too, and surreal, and sort of magical.

Perhaps it was the intimate, informal atmosphere, but Lillian gave the best reading I'd ever seen her do in the 20-whatever years I've known her.

Then I was off to Christian Bök's launch of *Eunoia*, his conceptual novel/poetry-thingy from Coach House Books. Christian's been around for a while now, mostly barking out L=A=N=G=U=A=G=E stuff, laughing real loud, and generally being a good alt-poetry citizen, and this book's been in the works for seven years. God, we were all sick of hearing about it.

The back of the Red Room (a recent addition to the trendy Chinatown/Kensington Market neighbourhood) was packed. Over a hundred people in a space meant for 30 or 40. The restaurant was so crowded you couldn't take off your coat without elbowing someone to the floor; and with your coat on, you sweated, turned red, and nearly fainted. There were TV cameras there, and people from the *Globe & Mail*, and tons of celebrities — Michael Ondaatje, André Alexis, Michelle Berry, Philip Monk, Andrew Pyper. People were air-kissing. It was terrifying. Why there was such a hubbub I dunno — something to do with networking skills, I guess.

After brief remarks from his publisher, Christian did his kinda Dadaist performance thing, a respectfully short reading from his book, which amused and delighted the gathered scenesters. I had read a bit of Christian's book and liked it lots, but I hadn't really bought his performances yet — technically brilliant but a little robotic. It was hot and crowded in there, like I said, and tough to get through to the bar for a life-saving cold beer. Pretty good spread of free grub, though (glad I didn't stuff myself with cookies at Lil's gig).

Yeah, this scene was about being seen, but it was also about support. (And it was a thrill when Christian made the front page of the *Globe*'s review section a couple weeks later. Avant-garde writing getting that kind of exposure. That can't be bad.) I was with my friends Daniel f. Bradley, a hardcore experimental poet who's anything but a scenester, and Anne McLean, a translator visiting from England. We sweated and coughed and hid in the corner, and Anne and I drank, then drank some more. We gazed upon the orgy of literary splendour and royalty, so far from a little room in the basement of a library a few kilometres away through the rain.

I knew I'd remember Lillian's reading a lot longer than I'd remember this one.

Oh, and something else about readings, and no, it's not how much I despise open mics — it's this new series, an occasional event at the Idler Pub called John & Daniel's Saturday Late Show. It's the most brilliant concept in readings in this city. One writer reads for as long as he or she likes. And organizers John Barlow (who thankfully doesn't host) and Daniel f. Bradley (who does) pick 'em right. jwcurry came in from Ottawa in November and read three half-hour sets — one as Wharton Hood, one solo, and one with various vocal accompanists. Best damn reading this town's seen in years.

Screw open mics. Screw the three-readers/20-minutes format. Screw some other stuff. Oh yeah, screw Harbourfront. Screw loudmouths. Host a reading in your living room. Next week.

January 2002

Christian Bök's Eunoia *went on to sell, oh, about 15,000 copies, making it likely the best-selling Canadian poetry book ever. Did it change the face of Canadian poetry? Make poetry popular again? Many thought the doors were now open for huge-selling books of poetry, and that they'd become rich and famous, and that poetry was as hip as pet rocks. But only Christian Bök became rich and famous. The rest of us shivered in our wet cardboard boxes, continuing to collect our annual negative royalty cheques when Chapters' ridiculously delayed returns came in.*

THE ONLY BOOKSTORE THAT MATTERS

I'M GETTING TO the end of my falafel — you know, where the tahini sauce starts dripping from the bottom of the wax paper and getting all over your hands and your $5 brogues from Goodwill. Anyway, I've just turned onto Harbord Street, near Bathurst, and I stumble across a new shop. A tiny place, not much bigger than my living room (which you've all been to, of course). The name of the shop is Spineless Literature.

I push open the door and I'm surrounded by shelves and racks of chapbooks. This is it — the small press bookstore I've dreamed of for years. Nick Power and I — after our successes with Meet the Presses and the Toronto Small Press Book Fair — once talked about opening such a shop in this very location.

The first shelf I browse is jammed with stuff — new books, old books, real old books. I see copies of Kevin Connolly's chapbook series from the '80s, Pink Dog Editions — poems and fiction by Daniel Jones, Tony Burgess, Gil Adamson, Greg Evason (where the hell is *he* now?), and even a copy of my own *Paralysis Beach*. Right next to those are about a dozen titles from Carleton Wilson's Junction Books. Carleton's one of the most prolific and devoted chappie publishers in Toronto, an anomaly in a scene crawling with tedious careerists gabble-blabbing about advances and agents and author photos.

A couple shelves down are some ziney books by Tara Azzopardi — quirky high-school-yearbook biographies accompanied by Tara's so-normal-they're-weird drawings. And there are some of Mark Connery's legendary *Rudy* comics, and an old newsprint comic book by Tuli Kupferberg of the Fugs. A little over are a stack of grotty photocopied pamphlets of visual poetry from Bob Cobbing's Writers Forum in England, and some Eternal Network emissions from Victor Coleman.

How come nobody told me about this place? I hear some rustling behind me and turn around. At a makeshift desk sits Jay MillAr; the place is volunteer-run, and this is his shift. Spineless Literature was his idea, and the hours are as erratic as the schedules of Jay's poet friends. When he closes up at seven tonight, the store won't open again till 3:17 the next morning, when John Barlow shuffles in and restocks the shelves with a bunch of pirated W.S. Merwin chapbooks he's been cranking out in editions of seven copies each. When Maggie Helwig arrives with her kid to open the shop again at noon, the door's unlocked, and John's sleeping on the floor. They get the coffeemaker going. They wait for customers. Doesn't matter how much they sell, because this tiny space is donated by the building's landlord, a closet haiku poet who doesn't really need the cash. But I'll empty my pockets here.

On the wall is a poster for a reading by Brian Dedora and Lynn Crosbie, both brilliant. I miss Brian since he moved to Vancouver a decade ago, and Lynn hasn't been published by a real small press in years, but she started out with a nasty little poetry zine called *Off the Pigs*. I figure you could cram about 20 people into this shop for a reading, sell beer from the bathroom. It's a good space, and I fantasize about running a poetry workshop here. I'll ask Jay about it another time.

Spineless Literature is the most important bookstore in Toronto. Nowhere else in this city are you going to find books by Jennifer Blowdryer and Opal Louis Nations and Daniel f. Bradley and Sandra Alland and Alfred Starr Hamilton and Laurie Fuhr and d.a. levy and X. Zivit 57 and Jim Smith and John M. Bennett and Paul Dutton and Dick Higgins and debby florence and Guy R. Beining and . . . I could go on but I won't.

This place is an education. Who cares about McClelland & Stewart's stinking spring poetry list? Here you can learn about your past — *Strange Faeces* and ganglia and Weedflower Press — and embrace a new generation of folders-and-staplers. Tell your agent, if you are fool enough to have one, to fuck off — you don't need her/him anymore, because there's no room for that crap in the world of the chapbook. This place is a slap in the face to Mike Harris and Jean Chrétien and McDonald's and Knopf and MuchMusic and Greg Gatenby and cellphones and Republicans and Indigo and all the other stops along the Axis of Evil. They can't kill it no matter what.

And not only because it doesn't exist.

March 2002

I still meet people who say they combed Harbord Street looking for Spineless Literature.

The dream of a small press bookstore hasn't abated, and Jay MillAr has partially fulfilled it with his travelling Apollinaire's Bookshop. At various literary events — notably the Lexiconjury reading series and his own innovative

Speakeasy — *Jay sets up a rack of portable shelves filled with a couple hundred titles that you just can't get anywhere else. Meanwhile, I'm doing Poetry Boot Camps in the upstairs gallery space at the excellent indie bookstore This Ain't the Rosedale Library.*

On Harbord Street, that spot that Nick Power and I dreamed of taking over 20 or so years ago is still vacant, its window plastered with posters for music clubs. After the revolution, it's ours.

RAZOVSKY AND ME

I TURNED OUT to be a writer and I got saddled with this name Ross. Lots of immigrant Russian names were shortened and anglicized back in the 1950s, and so Razovsky became Ross. But I could have been a Razovsky! Oh, the exoticness of those three syllables. My dad's parents were Razovskys and my mom's were Blatts. But I turned out to be a Jew named not only Ross, but also Stuart. Stuart Keith Ross, even. My grandfathers were Sam and Max. I'd take either of those first names, for sure. At least then, at my bar mitzvah, no one would have expected me to come marching through the congregation playing bagpipes.

Anyway, since my teens I'd threatened to change my name back to Razovsky. My parents felt awful — I was rejecting them and their choice to be Rosses. They'd blown it. So I hesitated. And then I began publishing. Soon the poetry chapbooks had piled up, and the novellas, all under the name Ross. Opal Nations had called me "Pods," and I imagined having "Pods Razovsky" splattered across my book covers. Now, that'd be something. In fact, I flirted with it a bit; my 1990 novella *Guided Missiles* is written by "Stuart Pods Ross."

Off and on through the 1990s, I wrestled with the idea of the name change. But I'd done so many readings and published so many chapbooks and ephemera as Ross, such a change would only confuse readers. A plan began to develop. I'd create a character named Razovsky, and star him in a sequence of poems, and I'd name a book after him. I'd have a book with "Razovsky" on the cover.

In the '90s, too, I began to write a bit about Jewishness, or about my Jewishness, anyway. It was something I'd avoided, though not consciously, all along. When my mom died in 1995, my Jewishness became more of a concern for me. I wrote a short story called "The Towel," about an old Jewish man who, post-operation, had a surgical towel left in him. And another one called "The Sun Tan," about old Jewish people in Florida. I thought it up while sitting around the pool at my parents' condo in Pompano Beach.

And then, by the turn of the century, my dad was very ill. The Razovsky poems started coming. My father — who never really got my poetry, but still loved to come to my readings — thought it was very funny that I wanted to use the name Razovsky on my third big book of poems. It always made him laugh. I explained to him how Razovsky was me and him and his father and all those really old bearded guys in the family photos on the wall, guys in Russia and Poland, some of whom wound up in concentration camps.

My dad died early in 2001; I had written four Razovsky poems: "Razovsky at Peace," "Razovsky at Night," "Razovsky on Foot," and "Razovsky Rides a Cloud." They felt like really Jewish poems. While I was sitting shiva for my father, I wrote another Jewish poem, called "After the Shiva." When *Razovsky at Peace* was published the following

30

September, I was sad that my dad hadn't lived to see it. In fact, I'd gotten the publisher to move its release forward a season to increase the chances. I almost read a Razovsky poem at the unveiling of my father's headstone (the unveiling for my brother Owen, who'd died suddenly six months before my father, was the same rainy summer day), but the poem was too weird, I think, and too surreal; it might freak the relatives. And we were already drenched to the skin. In the cemetery, I signalled to Rabbi Scheim that I wouldn't read the poem after all.

When I was a kid, I got called "dirty Jew" a lot. I had pennies thrown in my path. When I worked at a library up in North York, at Yorkdale Shopping Centre, and I charged people overdue fines, I was asked occasionally if I was "a Jew." When I sold my books on Yonge Street in the 1980s, a guy once threatened to flatten me because I wouldn't stand there and take his insults; he said he'd saved me from the fire in World War II and thus deserved my respect.

I don't go to synagogue much — mainly when someone gets married or when someone dies or when a friend's kid gets bar-mitzvahed. I like going, though — it's warm and communal, and I take comfort in the mournful tunes and all the old guys. I read along in Hebrew and have no idea what the words mean. My parents, Syd and Shirley, didn't go to synagogue much, either. But they'd have liked me to be a rabbi. They didn't mind that I was a socialist, and a poet, and an atheist. But couldn't I just be a rabbi, too?

Writing Razovsky poems is as close as I'll get to being a rabbi. It's my way of thinking about being Jewish. This character is going to be with me as long as I write poems. And I like him — I like Razovsky, even though he always beats the shit outta me at pinochle.

May 2002

Another Jewish poem I wrote after my mother's death is "The Monument," a pretty much true-to-life narrative about going with my dad to choose my mom's headstone at Goldberg Izenberg Monuments on Bathurst Street. Because we were looking at double headstones, my dad was also choosing his own. It was a horribly sombre experience, and very surreal. Which is perhaps why the poem itself isn't at all surreal.

And then there's "Selecting the Proper Casket," from 2003, which tells the story of the 14 hours after Owen's death. Because of various impending Jewish holy days, we had to bury my brother the day after he died. My father, my brother Barry, and I were still in shock when we found ourselves at Steeles Memorial Chapel, after a sleepless, grief-filled night, choosing Owen's casket.

"The Mud Above, the Sky Below," written around the same time, talks about the downtown Toronto neighbourhood my mother grew up in. Only three or four years old, and able to speak only Yiddish, she was pelted with snowballs on her way to school. The Snowball *is the title of a novel I've been working on for a couple of years, and it's pretty autobiographical, drawing on my own childhood in Bathurst Manor, a small suburban neighbourhood near the northern edge of Toronto. It's a tough one to write, and it might take a couple more research visits to a synagogue. Bring on the tartan yarmulkes!*

I DUCK FOR POETRY

I'M STANDING ON the corner of Charles and Yonge in downtown Toronto. It's a cold winter day, back when there used to be snow, in the mid-1980s. With gloved hands, I clutch a few of my self-published poetry and fiction chapbooks against a hand-written sign that's strung around my neck: "Writer Going To Hell — Buy My Books." I started doing this in 1979, and I'd continue until the early 1990s.

A big, tough-looking guy in his 20s walks by and calls me an asshole. I call him an asshole back. Whoops. He backtracks and puts his face up close to mine, while his buddy tries to drag him away. Even in this cold, I can smell stale smoke off his leather jacket. "What did you say?" he says.

"Well," I explain, "you called me an asshole, so I called you an asshole. But I'm sorry about that, I'm really tired, and, um . . ."

"I'm not from downtown," he sneers, as his friend tugs at his arm, tells him to forget it.

I interpret "not from downtown" to mean he's not gay. I try to defuse him, explaining how pathetic I am, etcetera, and he steps back, pauses, and suddenly takes a swing at me. I duck.

"Ducked," he says, and then he walks away.

Over the course of a dozen years, I sell 7,000 of my books at $2 to $5. Some days I sell only one or two; usually I sell six or seven; on Christmas Eve 1988 I sell 61 books. Crad Kilodney, the grandfather of literary street vendors, got me into this. During his 15 years on the street, he sold 35,000 books of his demented fiction, making him one of Canada's top-selling literary writers. A misanthrope to begin with, he became increasingly bitter and angry over those years. Last I saw him, a few years ago, he'd quit writing and was studying the stock markets 16 hours a day. He told me to buy Mongolian Gold in January and sell in June.

A middle-aged woman walks up and asks if I have any fiction. I show her my novella *Father, the Cowboys Are Ready to Come Down from the Attic.* I'm a little nervous as she opens it, because it's got some raunchy sex scenes, and she looks so nice and wholesome, so I try to distract her.

"Do you write, too?" I ask.

"Yes," she replies.

"Fiction?"

"Yes."

"Have you had anything published?"

"Yes . . ."

"Oh," I say, "what's your name? Maybe I've seen your stuff."

"Alice Munro."

She buys my book. I still hope she never tried to read it.

An older, stocky, bald guy walks up to me and asks what I'm doing. He asks if I pay my taxes, suggests that I'm cheating all honest folk like him, and threatens to knock my head off. I start to pack up my stuff, and he expresses glee. Not wanting to please him, I put my sign back on —

34

I'm going to stay put. He becomes more agitated and menacing. Frightened, I pack up my stuff and duck into Book City next door, where the staff all know me. He stands at the door and yells in, "I saved you from the fire in World War II, hook-nose!"

Down at Dundas and Yonge, a block from a couple of strip joints, I'm wearing the sign "Continuous Topless Poetry." A gangly guy in a stained T-shirt invites me for a coffee. I decline. He explains that I have a little man sitting on each of my shoulders; one is good and one is evil. Also, if I don't join him for a coffee, he will use his psychic powers to bring down the brick building I'm leaning against. It will make my head hurt. A couple weeks earlier, at this very corner, a guy threw another guy through the window of a Coles bookstore.

W.P. Kinsella walks up to me and asks if I know where Crad is. He doesn't so much as glance at my books before heading to the Burger King I point to. I hate his stupid, overwritten books anyhow. Arrogant schmuck — wannabe American. It drives me nuts when other writers stop and don't even look at my books. David Young stopped to say hi, but didn't buy a book. Earle Birney stopped and did. The one time I ever met him, and I think I muttered something embarrassing about "David."

I make some friends out there — a painfully skinny fellow named john curry who publishes weird little rubber-stamped poetry pamphlets. A teenager named Daniel Bradley who goes on to start his own small press a couple years later. A guy named Michael Dennis who wears a beret and writes like a Canadian Bukowski. A Chicago poet named Richard Huttel who's in town on his honeymoon and who'll become Toronto poetry's greatest American fan. I still know them, but there are so many others, too, friends from my years of selling on the street.

A pudgy man who looks like a D&D geek stops right in front of me. "You write these?" he asks.

I nod and hand him a copy of *When Electrical Sockets Walked Like Men*. He chats with me for a while, explaining that he's 3,000 years old. "You look good for your age," I tell him.

"Thanks," he replies.

I'm not out there anymore. It became pretty threatening on the street, and I felt bad taking business away from the growing number of panhandlers who needed the cash just to eat, or drink. Now I sell my books at readings and fairs, and a couple of presses publish me and put me in stores. But I miss that thing of meeting every single person who's going to read my poems and stories. I miss that family of random citizens.

July 2002

STOP BUGGING ME ALREADY!

THEY ASK ME, they ask me, they won't stop bugging me, they ask me, these little ones, what to do when they want to take their poems out of their desk drawers and make other people look at them. I could talk endlessly on that subject, and I do, but let's get it over with now, so I never have to deal with it again.

First thing: forget about making money, forget about big publishers, forget about agents. Over the 1990s, young writers largely became these bloat-brained monsters who think: *Career career career.* They don't think: *I wanna make a good poem; I wanna make a good story.* They want to get reviewed in the *Globe & Mail*, they want to appear on *Ziggy's Celebrity Literary Back Rub,* they want to have big shiny books, they want to eat dead snails and drink martinis with English-accented literary agents.

Next thing: read like crazy. There's no way you're going to write a good poem before you've read 500 other good poems, and lord knows it's nearly impossible to find 500 good poems, especially if you're some kind of raving literary nationalist. Read American poets from the 1960s and 1970s. Read a few Canadians from the same era. If you don't find a concrete image in the first three lines, throw the book out the window and pick up the next one. When you find something good, steal it. I mean, don't steal the actual words — steal how it's done.

OK, so you've read a bunch, and now you've learned how to steal, and thus write. Buy some literary magazines; buy some books. You'd better buy them if you expect anyone to buy *your* stuff. If you have to sacrifice a beer, so be it. Just spend your money on some good poems. When you've found a magazine that publishes poems you like, send them some of yours. Oh, don't forget to start your own magazine. And start your own press — you've got to start publishing little leaflets of your poems and chapbooks, because you've got to get the stuff into other people's hands. There's nothing shameful about self-publishing. What's shameful is to walk around gloating that someone else is publishing you, because all that means is that one other person on this whole lousy planet liked your stuff.

Here's a thing — did I say this yet? Hate older poets. Read older poets. Steal from them. Hate them some more. Read David McFadden. Hate him. But like his poetry. Read Bill Knott and Ron Padgett and Elaine Equi and Opal Louis Nations and Sharon Olds and James Tate and Lorine Niedecker and dear bill bissett. Then hate them, even if they seem lovable. (It's a ploy, anyway.)

Don't bother with creative writing workshops, unless I'm teaching them. Also, don't take creative writing at university. Take absolutely anything else, so you can learn about something useful, stuff like science and history that you can use in your poems. What's going to happen in a poetry workshop is all your worst tendencies are going to be encouraged, especially by all the other participants, and that's because they'll be godawful poets who write things like: "I'm lying on the beach. He walks

38

towards me. Will he be bold?" They'll ruin you. They'll make you write poems by committee. They'll destroy anything interesting in your lines.

Also, you've got to start going to readings. Listen to good poets, and bad ones. Pay attention: you're going to have to start doing readings yourself soon. You'll need to begin at open mics, probably; but I won't be there to cheer you on — open mics are way too painful. Watch how all the open-mic weasels leave right after they've read, without even sticking around for the feature reader. Make sure you stick around — not necessarily because the features are any good, but because, look, they had to suffer through *your* stuff.

You probably think I'm kidding, but I'm not. I mean all this. Stop phoning me up and asking how you can "become a poet." Read a 14-word poem by Nelson Ball. Look at where he puts his line breaks. Try to replace even one of his words — you can't do it. The damn thing is perfect. Worry about that — don't worry about reputation, or sales, or author photos, or launches. Write a 14-word poem that doesn't rhyme or contain the word *loneliness* or the word *I*. You'll be well ahead of the game.

September 2002

NO MERE MR. NICE GUY

I'VE DEVELOPED THIS reputation as a stand-up literary comic at readings. Even though it's my own fault, I'm still pissed off about it. I mean, sure there's humour in my poems, but I'm a serious writer. Audiences laugh at the funny stuff, but then they also laugh at the tragicomic stuff, too. I've been whining to my friends about this for ages. The prevailing theory is that audiences laugh because they're uncomfortable with my work and don't know how else to respond.

At the Harbourfront reading for ECW Press's 25th anniversary in October, I read two pieces — "Road Trip, Southern Ontario, 1999," an initially funny but ultimately sad poem about my father, and "Me and the Pope," a story about the pope stealing my girlfriend. I'm telling you, about 20 people approached me after the reading and every one of them said, "Great pope story. You were hilarious."

And then the next week, at Lexiconjury, I decided to do a "serious reading." I can't even remember the last time I didn't give in to the temptation to depend on the stuff people found funny (even if I didn't). Anyway, at Lexiconjury, I cracked a few jokes between pieces, and I read the pope story again, early in the set. But then I read some very serious poems, about my father's death, and about my brother Owen's death, and about the death of relationships. I felt really sombre. The applause was more measured than usual. Afterward, three people came up to me and said, "Fuck, that pope story was amazing."

*   *   *

For well over a year now, I've been agonizing over some other damn thing, too. Jack David, the publisher at ECW Press, came up with the ludicrous idea of putting out a hardcover book of my selected poems. I talked to my editor there, Michael Holmes: "Look, man, has my doctor told you something he hasn't told me? I'm way too young for a selected." And I argued, too, that my three spiney poetry books were all still in print, I hadn't won any awards, the masses weren't clamouring for more, and I didn't want my friends to have to fork out big cash for a hardcover book filled with poems they already had. Mainly, though, I just found the idea too embarrassing. Could we wait a few years and see what happens? Michael agreed.

Then I started second-guessing myself. Who'd turn down a hardcover selected? So I wrestled and complained and tortured myself. At the same time, I observed the enormous egos of writers I considered shitty. I started to think that maybe I was still so obscure after 25 years in the poetry racket because I was too modest. So, hoping to be convinced, I met up with Jack again and asked him why he wanted to do it — wouldn't it be absurd to publish a hardback selected by an unknown like me? "Yeah," he answered, "it's crazy. And that's why people will pay attention." So I said okay, I'll do it. And then I changed my mind back and forth over the next six months.

Yesterday, Michael called — did I want to do the selected this spring? He had to know by the end of the phone call, because they were about to print the spring catalogue. If I didn't say yes, I figured, I'd never have a hardcover book. Besides, if my publisher and editor thought it was a smart idea, who was I to argue? I capitulated. I told Michael it'd be called *Hey, Crumbling Balcony! Selected Poems & Some New Ones.* I'm finally looking at this writing thing as a career. It makes me uncomfortable.

*　　*　　*

What happens when a writer puts career before quality? rob mclennan's anthology *side/lines: A New Canadian Poetics*, that's what. I hesitated to write this, because rob would get mad at me, but then I remembered he already is.

rob's an Ottawa poet and literary organizer, and he puts tons of energy into the promotion of poetry, mostly his own. Since 1998, rob's put out *seven* books of poetry through various presses and about 50,000 of his own chapbooks. I don't like most of his poems — they all sound the same to me, and they're all about him. Also, he has this annoying propensity to dedicate his poems to other poets, or kick off his poems with a line from another poet. It comes off like so much name-dropping. There are, however, people who say rob mclennan is their favourite writer. I've *heard* them say it.

But back to the anthology, the sixth rob has edited, god save us. It's from Insomniac Press, who publish some books I love, but have a chronic typo problem. On the back cover of *side/lines*, rob's name is spelled wrong, and the word "refereshing" appears in the first line. In the table of contents, you get the letter "x" in place of page numbers, 31 times. rob's incomprehensible introduction, barely longer than a page, contains 19 typographical and grammatical errors.

That's just the beginning. The essays themselves, which presumably came from the contributors' electronic files, are in better shape, but far from error-free. Some of the essays are excellent, and some are a load, but either way, who's going to benefit from a rushed number like this?

Insomniac owes it to the contributors to pulp this edition, hire a new copyeditor and proofreader, slap rob upside the head for ignoring the proofs, and reprint the thing. As for rob: man, just stop publishing for five years and see where your poetry goes. You might get on to something good. You sure put in the sweat.

November 2002

Insomniac, who were the publishers of Word *when this column appeared, and, to their credit, didn't kill it, subsequently did issue a new, corrected edition of* side/lines. *Although it would be consistent with my nitpicky, snipey character to see if all these errors had been corrected, I never got around to doing that. rob was not pleased with this column, though I think it was pretty constructive. The thing that sparked the piece was the memory of sitting around in the hospitality suite of the Ottawa International Writers Festival a couple months earlier, with rob and jwcurry. rob was griping that he'd received the fourth set of proofs for his anthology and really didn't have time to read them. After all, he's a busy guy! I argued that the more sets of proofs you get to see, the better.*

Meanwhile, I'm still wrestling with this idea that I'm a hilarious poet. At readings, I often do "Road Trip, Southern Ontario, 1999," because it means a lot to me, and because it's sort of like keeping my dad alive in some way. But every time the audience laughs during the first half of the poem, I feel sort of guilty for

what's coming up, guilty that perhaps I'm being manipulative: "In two years, /
my father will be dead." And there are always one or two people in the crowd who
howl at that one. It's a real knee-slapper.

MAKE THE WRETCH PAY!

I HAD A blast the last couple of months as pencil-pusher in residence for the Writers' Circle of Durham Region. I had this spankin' big office in Ajax, about 40 minutes outside Toronto, and I sat behind a desk the size of Nunavut as writer after writer came in, and we talked about their work, and every last one of them was nice and interesting and enthusiastic, even the one guy in the suit. I always asked what they were reading, and in most cases, they listed exclusively Canadians. I was amazed.

I know Americans suck at a lot of stuff, like peace, justice, the environment, and brewing beer, but they sure produce a lot of good writers. Just finished reading *On the Level Everyday* (Talisman, 1997), a stimulating — if barely proofread — collection of talks by the late American poet Ted Berrigan. The more I read Berrigan, the more I'm reminded of the late Canuck poet bpNichol. They shared an incredible generosity of spirit, consistently encouraged young poets, loved bad puns, searched for the good stuff in whatever they read, were literary adventurers, and imbued their writing with their life and their life with their writing. They pretty much made their livings as poets. And they were both big guys who died way too young, Berrigan in 1983 and Nichol in 1988. If you like bp, check out Ted.

The segue here: making a living as a poet. My childhood friend Ken Shelson sent me a note the other day — his nine-year-old son Lee had written a school essay about one of my poems, "The Potatoes Are Crazy." Now, something's gotta be broken with the school system if they let little kids read poems about paranoid spuds, but here's how Lee's essay ends:

> *I chose this poem because the author is a friend of my father. He started writing poetry when he was very young, and now he's won all kinds of awards. He started selling his poetry on Yonge Street. Stuart used to type up his poems and photocopy them and sell them for a dollar. He drew most of the pictures by himself. Now his books are published by real publishers and he has real illustrators doing the pictures. He is not rich.*

Lee's taken some licence with the facts (I've never won an award, though Alistair MacLeod stole the Trillium from me), but we won't dock him any grades for that. The kid scored one direct hit: poets don't get rich. Perhaps that's because we do way too much for free, and people come to expect it of us. It bugs me when bars hold readings, and the feature writers — who draw in the audience who drink beer and eat — get nothing for their efforts. Manny at the Idler used to offer a $15 food/bar tab for each reader, a nice gesture (though I was bugging him to up it to $25 just before he closed the bar). I recently read at Lexiconjury, for free, and had to buy my own beverages. I gave the organizers grief, just as I did the LitLive folks in Hamilton who pay nothing and let you buy your own drinks.

And at the I.V. Lounge Reading Series, back when poet Paul Vermeersch was hosting, I started my reading by griping about the lack of a free drink, the least I could get for reading for zilch. I said it real loud, because the owner had ducked into the back room. Vermeersch generously offered to buy me a pint out of his own pocket and I turned him down: why should he have to pay? The place was packed and only the bar was making any money. Thereafter, I.V. readers got two drink tickets each. (Reportedly the Lex has also since changed its cheapass ways.)

But it's not just organizers and bar owners who are responsible. I'd say most people who come out to readings spend more on beer than on poetry books. And if asked to contribute to the passed hat, they'll toss in a toonie, then spend a fin on a Ratsass Cream Ale. Here's the rule from now on: you give the reader at least as much as you spend on a beer. And poets oughta boycott any series that doesn't pony up cash or the equivalent. Let's stop devaluing our own work. Let's stop being so fucking grateful that someone asked us to read or published our poem. Let *them* be grateful.

I do this column for free, too, though I get to plug my career in italics at the end each time. But over the past few months I've asked for a complimentary subscription, so I don't have to forage for a copy of *Word* on the first of the month. The publisher still hasn't gotten it together. I mean, I write 750 words for free every 60 days, and he can't cough up a stinkin' 75-cent stamp to mail me a copy? I feel strongly about this — strongly enough to declare this installment my last.

But then I'd be giving up the ability to torment *Word*'s publisher right here in his own magazine.

January 2003

My complimentary subscription to Word *began with the next issue. A few months later, I told my editor, Maria Erskine, that I couldn't keep doing this for free and that perhaps it was time to pull the plug on "Hunkamooga." I mean, even if I got a lousy $25 a column I'd at least feel an effort was being made to compensate me. She hinted discreetly that some changes were on the horizon and that I should consider sticking around. With dreams of $25 per column ($150 a year!) dancing in my head, I agreed to hang in till September. The big change turned out to be that Bev Daurio of the Mercury Press was buying* Word. *She did, and the magazine expanded and improved and looked a lot better. New columnists came on board, a new energy revitalized the thing. I continue to write my column for free, though now I get a business-card-size ad whenever I want one. If I stick it into a whole-wheat bun, add pickles and ketchup, I've got myself a burger!*

THE GREAT CBC POETRY
DEATH MATCH

BY THE TIME you read this, I will have either won or lost the first round of CBC Radio's National Poetry Face-Off contest. Me, I'm putting my money on those who are not me. A few weeks back, the CBC commissioned five Toronto poets (as well as five more from each of 11 cities across the country) to write a poem on the theme of escape. The poem was to be no longer than four minutes, and it would be vetted for language, since you can't say "poo" on radio, I guess.

It all sounded very spoken-wordy to me. My poet friend Clint Burnham in Vancouver calls that stuff "shouted word." George Bowering, Canada's first poet laureate, recently called it "horseshit" and said he was disgusted by the concept of competitive poetry. Where do I stand? Before this contest, I'd never even attended a slam. To me it sounds like a recipe for bloated egos and really bad poetry delivered in a tone usually reserved for threatening to punch out someone's lights.

But I liked the theme — escape — and the money sounded pretty good, even if I didn't win. All the competitors would get paid for broadcast rights. So I took up the challenge, grumblingly, and began my poem about escape. I groused a bunch at the contest producer's guidelines. Sentences should be short and punchy, they said, whereas mine are usually long and rambling. Performances should be zippy and charismatic, whereas I often veer towards the whiney and mopey. The poem should be gettable on a single listen and not need repeated readings. Hell, sometimes I don't get my own poems till years after I write them. If I get them at all. The nice CBC folks assured me, though, that they liked my stuff, and I should proceed as I normally would. But keep in mind it's for radio, they said, again and again.

Now, in addition to reading our entry poem, we contestants also have to read a "warm-up" poem of no more than two minutes. And we have to read the final draft of our entry poem into the voicemail of the CBC producer. This is not the way I normally write poetry or do readings. Maybe this is the life of the spoken-word poet. The CBC website says I'm one of five of "Toronto's hottest spoken-word performers." Yikes.

In a few days, I'll read my poem, "Do Not Ask Where I Started," in front of a couple hundred people at a Toronto bar. And Margaret Christakos will read hers, and also Jacob Sheier and Jemini and Seth-Adrian Harris. Then everyone'll vote by secret ballot for their favourite poem or favourite person or favourite haircut or whatever.

Like I said, I don't expect to win. But I'd like to win. Does that make me competitive? At any reading I give, I don't like to get overshadowed, even by my best friends. When I read on the same bill as the American fictioneer Gordon Lish a few years ago at the Ottawa International Writers Festival, I hated that he eclipsed me, even though he's one of my favourite writers. I really don't want to admit that that makes me competitive, but maybe it does.

I know that when I apply for a grant, I'm competing. And I know that competition often guides the kinds of projects that people apply with: go ethnic, go family roots, go gender politics, and your chances of getting a grant seem to increase. Hell, I write poems about poodles — where does that leave me? Well, if I want a grant, I better write poems about the poodle immigrant experience.

The winners of the first round of the Face-Off in each city go up against each other on CBC Radio One, and then there'll be a phone-in vote. The winner will be carried through towns and villages on the spry shoulders of Jean Chrétien (or perhaps Dick Cheney, if the U.S. annexes us by then because we don't hate Saddam Hussein enough).

But after the competitive dust has settled, I have a plan. I've accumulated a great stack of poetry books over the past few months — stuff by Dean Young and Bill Knott and Carolyn Forché and Charles Simic and Frederick Seidel — and I'm really just looking forward to lying in bed till noon every day, eating potato chips and reading it all. And reading it will make me write, and I'll look at what I've written and say, "That's some weird shit I write." And that's what writing poetry is all about.

March 2003

THE TRUTH IS
UNBECOMING (OF ME)

WHEN WE LAST met, I was spewing quasi-venom about the CBC National Poetry Face-Off, in whose Toronto contest I was a competitor. I was convinced I would not win, and I dissed the thing. And then, a few days after I handed in my column, I won. My poem, commissioned on the theme of escape, is called "Do Not Ask Where I Started."

I admit — although I am against the idea of competitive poetry — it made me happy to win. The night was fun, and I met some neat people. And then I began to want to win the national finals. I was never confident, but I was sure hopeful. Figured it might open a door or two for me — there *are* people in positions of power out there who believe such things matter. So maybe I'd get into a literary festival or something.

About an hour ago, the winner of the nationals was announced. It was not me. And I shall not be gracious in defeat. The winner was retired schoolteacher Mary T. Macdonald, whose first line contained the word "conventionality." She's from Edmonton, she's 83, and she talks in her poem a lot about gardening and — appropriately enough — mortality. And she didn't even write a commissioned poem: she just cobbled together two already-written poems. She said so in her victory interview. She obviously struck a chord — among those who buy poetry books by Jimmy Stewart.

I thought I was gonna win with a surreal poem about a guy who falls in love with a tornado? A poem that evokes poodles, Heidi Fleiss, and Underwood manual typewriters? Well, I'm back on earth, where I recognize that I do — as I pointed out in my last column — write weird shit. Would victory have been a vindication of my crusade for absurdity in poetry? Or a sign that I was getting soft in my middle age? Look at Christian Bök: his clever exercise in vowel withdrawal wins the Griffin, and now, rumour has it, the guy's writing *Beachcombers* episodes.

Christian! The series ended two decades ago!

*   *   *

While bashing grandmothers is a great way to win reader sympathy, I'd best move on to other topics. Like the Toronto Small Press Book Fair. At the last three or four fairs, it felt like the local small press scene was coming to life again. Some of the old geezers like me were still there, sure, but also lots and lots of new presses, run by brave young freaks. Maria Erskine and Maggie Helwig, who have helmed the fair for the past five years, had dragged it out of the doldrums, making it visible again on Bloor Street and digging up a public in huge new numbers. But there's something, too, about their profoundly modest and committed spirits, their generosity; stuff like that is contagious.

Well, the two M's have stepped aside, at the top of their game, and two new coordinators are running the show this spring: Kristiana Clemens —

cartoonist, wacky DJ, zinester, and indie media activist; and Beth Follett
— novelist, poet, and publisher of the elegant Pedlar Press. These women
will bring a different energy to the fair, I'll bet, but an equally positive
one. A couple of substantial changes are already in place: no to an instant
anthology this time around, but yes to an after-fair reading at the Victory
Café.

So come to the fair! And start up a poetry mag, you lazyass! Buy lots
of chapbooks! Visit my table and find out who Bill Knott is!

*   *   *

Hey, I've lived in Toronto all my life, and I sometimes forget there are living literary communities outside the gruesomely hip urban jungle. Had
the educational pleasure of reading in two such venues recently. It's the
best kind of reading — reading to a whole new audience.

In April, I got the royal treatment at the annual Words in Whitby festival.
I couldn't believe I was slated to read at *10 a.m.* on a Saturday morning,
along with a bestselling author of werewolf novels. But to my astonishment,
over a hundred people showed, and I got a near-standing ovation and sold
heaps of books. I stayed for most of the three-day hoedown, hanging with
old VIA Rail Cross-Canada Writers' Tour pals Sarah Dearing and
Rabindranath Maharaj and making lots of new friends. And the bonus:
during David Adams Richards' fantastic reading, something he said
triggered for me exactly how to begin this novel that's been kicking around
in my head for years.

And one Sunday back in March, poet and porn-soap-maker Jen
LoveGrove and I drove the treacherous, icy roads to Elora — musta been
25 below — to read at Gordon Gilhuly's Café at the End of the Universe
series. A dozen or so locals came out on that dark and crappy night. They

were curious but welcoming, and it was like no Toronto reading I've been to. Gilhuly was a brilliant host. When one shy open-mic poet said she'd written her poem in a Chinese restaurant, he responded, "That's the thing about writing a poem in a Chinese restaurant — 10 minutes later you want to write another."

May 2003

EVERYTHING REVOLVES AROUND ME, I TELL YOU!

HOW SELF-ABSORBED can I get in this column? Just keep reading.

Last week ECW Press threw a launch party for their spring poetry titles: Jacqueline Turner's *Careful*, Gil Adamson's *Ashland*, and my own *Hey, Crumbling Balcony! Poems New & Selected*. Leaving aside (for now) the roiling hell that occurred behind the scenes over the production of my book, which nearly wasn't ready in time, the launch was a huge success. The Gladstone Hotel Ballroom is a great venue, and the place was packed with over 200 people; more than 100 books were sold; the food from Shanghai Cowgirl was excellent; there was right-on live jazz with the trio Jennifer, Greg, and Wally; and people seemed to have a good time.

A lot of writers talk about the devastating post-launch plummet. The book is out; the world hasn't changed; what is there to look forward to now? I never get that — I'm pleased as a black ant on a writer's ankle (I just shook one off) that my book is out, and it's a beautiful thing, physically: a hefty hardcover designed by Dana Samuel, with a traffic-stopping shiny blue jacket populated by my hand-drawn poodles. (My hero Ron Padgett ends his poem "Post-Publication Blues" with: "Unfortunately I am a very bad poet and / the book is no good.") I have no illusions about changing the world, and I have a lot to look forward to. I'm too busy to feel empty. I expect only pitiful sales and no attention, though I hope for better.

But the launch: it's a weird thing for sure. It evokes in me a mixture of exhilaration and frustration. And the next day: guilt. I was thrilled that so many people came, thrilled and grateful. I got to speak with some of them for a couple of minutes, some for just a few seconds, and some I only saw out of the corner of my eye, but never spoke with. For me the launch is a three-hour block of interrupted conversations and panicked cross-the-room waves, punctuated by a short reading. I become a rabid monkey swinging from vine to vine through the room, never sitting down. I feel some compulsion to play host, make sure everyone's got a chair, everyone's got a drink.

I can't get the hang of the Lynn Crosbie Launch Method: at the recent grotesquely star-studded jamboree for her incredible (but ugly) new M&S poetry book, *Missing Children*, she held court at a table to the side, sur-rounded by family, close friends, and bodyguards, and let people come to *her*. That's so sensible. But I can't do it.

Anyway, the next day, I've got regrets and guilt like I'm hungover, but I'm not hungover. I think of all the people who came to the launch who I didn't greet, didn't thank. Hell, some people drove all the way from Whitby. Then I start thinking about all the people who didn't show up, people I wish had been there. I wish dear David McFadden had come, but his invitation showed up in his mailbox too late. I wish my brother had showed, my own brother — our family is just me and him, after all — but he didn't see it as important, I guess. I did the weird thing of tracking down friends from public school, people I haven't seen in 20 years, and sending them invites — Sid Radomski (who shows up in my poem "Little Black Train"), Murray Nightingale (whose dad owned a slaughterhouse), Benjie Murray (I called him "Spongy"). They were probably off playing pinochle in somebody's suburban rec room.

But my parents' best friends, Anne and Stan, dropped by the launch and bought my book and had me sign it for them. Anne told me, "I think about your parents every day." I wish my parents had been there, but they're dead, which is a pretty good excuse for not showing up. I knew, though, that Anne and Stan were there on their behalf, to make sure I was doing OK. I got weepy and ducked away.

To my astonishment, Jim Smith turned up, with his partner, Jo-Anne McNamara. Jim was once a close, close friend, and my favourite poet, but when he suddenly left the literary world to become a lawyer, we had a nasty falling-out. Last time I'd seen him was at the wake for the science-fiction writer Judith Merril six years ago, where we agreed we oughta keep in touch before one of us died without any goodbyes. Much hugging ensued. See ya in 2009, Jim!

Tom Walmsley, another long-lost friend and literary hero, but one I've recently renewed contact with, turned up as well, with Pam Stewart. Pam and her kids used to publish the zine *Dysfunctional Family.* Tom, of course, wrote a heap of great plays, a couple of books of raw poems, and the legendary punk novel *Doctor Tin.* He's been underground for a decade: it was good to have him there. We will all go out and buy his new novel, *Kid Stuff,* from Arsenal Pulp in the fall. I've read it, and it's going to be a classic.

But enough about Tom and Jim and Spongy; let's talk about me some more.

I've become a difficult author. I was just on the phone with Tracey from ECW a second ago. I asked her if I'm considered difficult around the office. She sidestepped the question three times, and that was all the confirmation I needed. Yeah, I've been a little demanding about certain things this time around, but that's how it is when you hit your fourth book with the same publisher. You think that somehow things might be different, so you start getting controlling. I realized I was a difficult author just the other day, when I was in ECW's Beaches office and saw the stack of press releases for my new book. It read across the top, in big letters, "*Hey! Crumbling Balcony.*" But the title is actually *Hey, Crumbling Balcony!* I asked them to redo it, because the punctuation is important. They happily obliged. But still, it came over me like a wave, like a mudslide. *They hate me here. My publisher hates me.*

How can I live with this thing of being a difficult author? I make my living as an editor, and I dread difficult authors. Oh my god, I dread myself!

July 2003

OK, here's a little dirt on the near-disaster of Hey, Crumbling Balcony! *But only a little dirt. Buy me some crappy red wine at the Victory Café and I'll tell you the rest.*

As so often happens, the book got a little more behind in its editorial and production schedule, every step of the way — beginning with me. Anyway, a few days before the launch, ECW poetry editor Michael Holmes told me the book might not be ready. In the course of our conversation, accusations and nasty words flew. It was tense and ugly. It unfolded over the next couple of days that the printer would actually hand-bind as many books as they could over the weekend and send them in by bus. So the 21 copies of my book that made it to the launch — in fact, got to Toronto mere hours before the launch — were a special edition.

ECW pre-sold signed copies of the regular edition at the launch, and when the books finally came in, I popped into the office and inscribed them. I hand-

delivered about 20 of the books, which was sort of fun, and the rest were mailed. I bet Jacqueline Susann never had to do that.

HOW'S YER SMALL PRESS BRAINS?

I'M TIRED. I CAN'T come up with a column. I feel like I've bitched about everything there is to bitch about. I really wanna spend the next 800 words complaining about open mics again, because I sat through yet another painful — *horrible!* — one the other week at the Art Bar reading series, but I've already travelled that gravel road. I could do one of those nice columns where I say nice stuff about someone and celebrate the Wonderful Community That Is the Small Press World, but I'm feeling pretty grumpy, even though I enjoyed the recent blackout.

So here's a quiz for you. The topic is small presses and small pressers. The first person to turn in a complete set of correct answers wins. If no one manages that, then the highest score — first received — gets the prize. The prize is me, in your living room, giving a reading, but only if you live in the GTA. (I'm pretty busy in October, but I'll come over to your place and do the reading in November if you win. Please have a glass of water ready for me.)

1) The brilliantly named Strange Fæces Press was the project of what British-born writer and doo-wop DJ who I idolize?

2) What the heck was the name of that literary magazine that David McFadden edited back in the 1960s when he was barely an adult?

3) Name three imprints or magazines associated with the jwcurry empire.

4) What year did the first Toronto Small Press Book Fair — founded by Nick Power and me — take place and where did it happen?

5) Name six poets associated with the New York School. And if you haven't read them, you better get to it or else how the hell do you expect to ever write a good poem?

6) What sound-poetry ensemble did local troublemaker Paul Dutton once belong to? Oh yeah? And what about 'pataphysician Michael Dean?

7) This Toronto micropress has published chapbooks by Lynn Crosbie, Michael Dennis, and Kathy Shaidle. What's the press and who runs it?

8) *Shloodo Shlaada* editor Joe O'Sullivan published poems in what nut?

9) He is a poet and bookseller, and she is a visual artist who collaborated with bpNichol, and they live in Paris, Ontario, where the rivers Grand and Nith meet. Who are they?

10) What four magazines have I published under my Proper Tales Press imprint?

11) Crad Kilodney, the granddaddy of Toronto literary street vendors and one-time porn-magazine advice columnist ("Dear Reverend Kilodney"), published dozens of his absurdist fiction books through his own Charnel House. But what three Canadian presses cranked out Crad's other books?

12) Jack David (in Toronto) and Robert Lecker (in Montreal) run ECW Press. What in god's name does ECW stand for?

13) Once upon a time, Silas White's Nightwood Editions and Bev Daurio's The Mercury Press were other presses. Name those presses or I won't read in your living room.

14) Name eight writers published by Kevin Connolly's now-defunct Pink Dog Press. And if you see Kev, bug him to start up his new magazine already, because he won't listen to *me*.

15) Brit poet Bob Cobbing kicked the bucket recently. What was his preferred medium for his visual work?

16) The head honcho of Coach House Books published a novel I liked a lot. Name honcho and novel.

17) The great American poet Bill Knott (whose most recent book, *Lessons from the Orphanage and Other Poems*, I published, and which you should order from me through hunkamooga.com)

collaborated with what Pulitzer Prize winner on what weird little novel?

18) Meredith Quartermain and Jacqueline Turner are responsible for what important West Coast literary website?

19) What Jewish-Canadian poet wrote the immortal visually winding line "th' bees bring home th' groceries, th' groceries, th' groceries"?

20) Charlie Huisken, co-owner (with Dan Bazuin) of the fine indie bookstore This Ain't the Rosedale Library, wrote for the now-defunct arts mag *Only Paper Today* under what excruciatingly clever pseudonym?

21) The Black Mountain poets were a huge influence on the Canadian poets who published what West Coast mag in the 1960s? Oh, and what similarly titled magazine did Toronto's D.M. Owen and Norman Chadwick start publishing in the 1980s?

22) What kind of warfare did the late Pulp Press fictioneer D.M. Fraser, one of this country's great unrecognized literary treasures, write about?

23) What gay American poet and novelist is fixated on teen pop superstar Leif Garrett?

24) Back when he was alive, which is what he should be still, but isn't, Hamilton-born poet and fiction-writer Daniel Jones ran an

excellent chapbook series. What was his imprint called and where did he stick the CN Tower?

25) Margaret Atwood's first book was eight pages long. What was it called and who published it?

September 2003

You'll find the quiz answers at the back of this book. I sure hope they're right. And, even though the contest's over, if you want me to come and read in your living room, I'm sure we can work something out.

THE COMFORT OF MISERY

I'VE BEEN WONDERING for a few months now why I find this column increasingly difficult to write. It occurred to me this afternoon, as I was peering out into cloud-enshrouded mountains from Banff, that perhaps it's simply that I have less to gripe about than I did a couple years ago. Or maybe I just *feel* less like griping. Nah, I've griped plenty in recent weeks — just ask my publicist at ECW.

But things are going pretty good with my literary life. I'm in Banff right now, winding down for a few days after WordFest: Banff-Calgary International Writers Festival. I've met some great small pressers here, including novelist Wayne Arthurson from Edmonton and poet Ali Riley from Nelson. Wayne is officially the nicest guy in Canadian writing, and Ali sings Hank Williams like she's wearing his shoes. They're good writers, too, and now they're my friends. I bumped into Toronto poet and rocker Robert Priest on the plane out here, and I always enjoy hanging around with him. I don't know if he remembers the vicious review I wrote of one of his books in *Mondo Hunkamooga* 15 years ago, but he's won me over by now anyway. Australian novelist Joan London belongs to a whole other breed of writers, and she and her husband, the non-writer Geoff, get voted the most charming people in Alberta.

Festival "artistic associate" Ian Samuels, a poet who's pushing aside his own literary ego to pretty much run this show, lines me up with a poetry workshop for about 40 kids from the B.C. interior who've been bussed in to experience a literary festival. These kids are amazing and they write some amazing poems.

The other week I was living in the hospitality suite of the Ottawa International Writers Festival. In fact, I was the Poet in Residence there. What that means is that I slept in the hospitality suite and ordered beer and sandwiches for the next day as things wound down at three or four in the morning, and I gathered up all the beer bottles and sandwich crusts so Housekeeping wouldn't catch on to the fact that writers are disgusting slobs. Means, too, that I pinch-hit on occasion, like stepping into George Bowering's shoes to host the Talonbooks anniversary reading when George wrecked himself breaking up a dogfight.

Actually, I stay in the festival's hospitality suite every year, whether or not I'm actually participating in the readings. I do not know exactly how I earned this magical privilege, but I've generally considered this to be the highlight of my literary year, and I'm really good at ordering sand-wiches.

I spend an afternoon wandering the National Gallery with David McFadden, a nice way to pass time with my favourite Canadian poet. McFadden's like my New York School heroes: he knows a lot of painters. Tells me tales of Greg Curnoe, as we note there's only one Curnoe on display right now. He tells me tales of William Ronald, an abstract painter who I remember as the host of an insane local TV show called *Free for All* back when I was a kid. For the first time, I check out the really old stuff

— the pre-20th-century. Hey, they did good stuff then, too! Done with art, David and I head to the War Museum, where David tells me about the Fenians. We watch cool old newsreels. In every gallery, the guards or ticket-takers are very talkative. McFadden attracts this. He talks to everybody. I realize I'm no longer intimidated by David, maybe because I'm older than I once was, so I can talk to him like a normal person.

Among the many great people I meet in Ottawa is Melanie Little, a very cool fiction writer who is being hailed as the next Alice Munro. I like her stories more than Munro's, and I worry about the "next Bruce Springsteen" syndrome. That's a lotta pressure. Melanie's husband, Peter Norman, is a quirky guy and interesting writer, too. He knows everything about every movie ever made. I also get to spend some time with poet David O'Meara, who is officially the nicest guy in Canadian writing. His new book, *The Vicinity*, has a really poignant poem about King Kong.

Derek McCormack came in from Toronto and gave a killer reading from his new novel, *The Haunted Hillbilly*, at the National Library and Archives of Canada. The woman who introduced him, a local chief librarian, introduced Derek at length, quoting the voluptuous praise of many writers. After the reading, she gave Derek her research — a thick sheaf of printouts from the Internet. Turns out she'd confused him with Eric McCormack.

And then there's Pablo Armando Fernández. He is known in Cuba as "el Poeta." I don't know if this is a compliment, as it evokes homogeneity. He writes these abstract, philosophical poems, sorta Cubist, which is interesting for a Cuban. Pablo places his hand on my shoulder and his bulbous snout three inches from mine. "I am your father; you are my son," he says through his thick accent. (Actually, he's not my father; my father is two years' dead and I still dream about him nearly every night.)

"Don't laugh! This is *serious*! Don't look away! I am your *father*." In the hospitality suite, much whisky within him, he points at random writers: "Take off your shoes!" he commands. He says that feet are very important. Without them, we couldn't walk. He is officially the craziest guy in Cuban writing.

And in that hospitality suite, for once I don't argue with rob mclennan, though at one point I do kick him in the foot, my contribution to Canadian literary criticism.

My readings in Ottawa went really well, and I also led a poetry boot camp that had a *waiting list*. In Calgary/Banff, I fucked up my first reading by trying to be too entertaining, but redeemed myself in my second reading by being depressing. Depressing always cheers everyone up.

Other good things:

• Just before I left for Ottawa, I met up with Julie Crysler, editor of *This Magazine*, and accepted the position of literary editor for the new year. Now I can reject all my friends who submit stuff and they will hate me.
• George Murray gave my book *Hey, Crumbling Balcony! Poems New & Selected* a rave review in the *Globe & Mail*. George and I have a tempestuous relationship, so it was nice of him to set his contempt for me aside, or is it my contempt for him? In my travels, I've met a couple of strangers who bought my book because of that review. I'm beginning to accept the concept that there are people I do not know who have bought my books.
• I've been leading a lot of poetry workshops lately, and it's going well. My imposter syndrome is subsiding.
• I'm working on a novel, and I think I'm actually going to finish this one. It will be published and sell only 247 copies, but I'll still be happy.
• Ron Padgett and Bill Knott exist, and so does James Tate. Three good

reasons not to obliterate the United States of America. (Also, it would probably smell up Canada if we did that.)

There are lots more good things in my literary life, too, but this column is tedious enough already. Besides, I'm sure everything's going to collapse soon, and then I can once again luxuriate in the comfort of misery.

* * *

The winner of last column's contest, culled carefully from the two brave contestants who actually sent in their answers, is Susan Helwig, who correctly answered a bunch of my questions about the small press universe. Susan wins a reading by me in her living room.

November 2003

A year later, I got replaced in the Ottawa International Writers Festival's hospitality suite — by rob mclennan, my arch-nemesis. It really smarted. I mean, I knew I wasn't actually entitled to the honour, but still. And after all those years of clearing up beer bottles and cigarette butts, stray broccoli fragments and sandwich crusts, and after I'd raised $500 for the festival in a fundraising workshop in 2003. Was it because I kicked rob? Was it because I told off some other local poet for freeloading and necking with his girlfriend in the suite? Was I getting way too proprietary about the space?

What makes the Ottawa festival so magical is its organizers, father-and-son team Neil and Sean Wilson, and Kira Harris. Their enthusiasm is so genuine and their approach so grass-roots and unbureaucratic. I've been to the Toronto festival (as audience) a bunch of times, and the writers are kept up in Pedestalville there — fans get to see them close-up only in the book-signing lineup; in Ottawa, the organ-

izers have created an atmosphere where writers and readers mix, where you might actually get a chance to raise a pint or have a chat with an author you admire.

Anyway, Kira says I got the boot because the festival board decided to make the hospitality-suite position a rotating one, and because she thought I didn't want to do it anymore. Kira and Sean are practically family to me, but I suspect she's protecting me from an uglier truth. Anyway, I couldn't even bear to attend the 2004 festival, though it meant missing S.E. Hinton (that's right! S.E. Hinton!) and a sonnet duel by Peter Norman and Stephen Brockwell, and hanging out with Michael Dennis and other Ottawa pals.

If any other festival would like to install me in their hospitality suite, well, I'm available. I promise not to kick anyone. Unless they deserve it.

TEEN POETS TAKE TULSA!

I'M WONDERING IF he folded and stapled this very copy. Or maybe Joe did. And how in hell did they snag Jack Kerouac?

My apartment is bursting with books, and with small press magazines, chapbooks, leaflets, postcards, and ephemera. I have perhaps the largest Strange Fæces collection in Canada. But my immersion in the work of the New York School of Poets over the past decade led me to a prize item: *The White Dove Review,* the magazine Ron Padgett launched when he was in high school in Tulsa, Oklahoma, in 1959, the year I was born.

I'd read about this magazine, but doubted I'd ever see a copy. On a whim, I punched in the title in an online used-book service. And there it was: the very first issue, for only $5 Yankee, from a bookseller who presumably didn't know any better. A week later, I held the stapled 16-page chapbook in my hands. It was even more exciting than when I'd got my paws on the first four hefty issues of *Locus Solus*, the early-'60s organ of the New York School put out by John Ashbery, Kenneth Koch, Harry Mathews, and James Schuyler.

I don't know too much about how *The White Dove Review* came to be. Padgett was editor, Dick Gallup (then called Richard) was managing editor, and Joe Brainard (whose *The Friendly Way* I later reprinted through my Proper Tales Press) and someone named Michael Marsh were the art editors. The first issue contains poems by Padgett, Clarence Major, Paul Blackburn, Vernon Scannell, Jack Kerouac, Simon Perchik, and Kitsano Katue. There are also drawings — all portraits — by Brainard, Marsh, and John Kennedy. I can barely recognize Brainard's work, but even at about 17 years old, Padgett already had that Padgett sound. Here's the ending of his poem "Bartok in Autumn": "nature / is merely passive violence / and air." See what I mean?

I wrote to Padgett, who I think thinks I'm a crazed stalker, and he filled me in a bit on the magazine, which lasted five issues. After No. 2, apparently, Gallup and Marsh graduated from high school, and Betty Kennedy came on board. The magazine ceased when Brainard and Padgett escaped Tulsa after their own high school careers came to an end. Among the writers who appeared in the puny *White Dove Review* were giants like Allen Ginsberg, Ted Berrigan, LeRoi Jones, Gilbert Sorrentino, Fielding Dawson, and Peter Orlovsky.

You can tell, by the tedious list of names I've just inflicted on you, how obsessed I am. So here's an anecdote from David Lehman, relating the birth of the second generation of the New York School in his excellent book *The Last Avant-Garde*: "[It] got its start on the day in 1959 that [Ted] Berrigan, an army veteran majoring in English at the University of Tulsa, walked into the bookstore where Ron Padgett, then still a high school student, worked part-time. Berrigan was accompanied by a girlfriend, Pat Mitchell; Padgett told them about the literary magazine he and his pals had launched, *The White Dove Review*. Berrigan bought a copy . . ." I like that Berrigan forked over the 25 cents for the mag, encouraging the young pups.

Padgett writes in his lovely *Ted: A Personal Memoir of Ted Berrigan*: "I was a junior in high school . . . I had started a little magazine, which the owner of the bookstore encouraged me to sell in the store. I displayed it in a modified cigar box. The next time I came to work after meeting Ted, I found some typewritten poems folded lengthwise and stuck in the box. It was a manuscript from Ted, along with a cover note."

So they became buddies, and later Padgett married Pat, Brainard became a major American artist, and Berrigan (the American bpNichol) drank a lot of Pepsi and ripped the sonnet a new asshole. Oh, and Ron Padgett went on to write the poems that made him my favourite poet (which is, of course, his most prestigious accomplishment).

In my 1989 poem "Ladies & Gentlemen, Mr. Ron Padgett," Ron comes to Toronto and we grab a burger at the now-defunct Toby's at Church and Wellesley, the city's gay ghetto. Padgett goes for the bill at the end of our visit, and I grab it from him, then realize I forgot my wallet at home: "The waitress would say, / 'Don't worry about it. / This is Mr. Ron Padgett.' // And everyone'd turn their heads." In my imaginary stalkerish world, every Torontonian knew Padgett's work. Which is as it should be.

My copy of *The White Dove Review* is in pretty good condition, considering. A little yellowed and a little worn, but if I rub my fingertips over the cover I can just about feel a few residual molecules of the fingertips of... Well, I can't exactly make it out, but I'm thinking it's Padgett. Those are some very fine molecules.

January 2004

The origins of The White Dove Review *are given more detailed context in Ron Padgett's extraordinary and hefty* Joe: A Memoir of Joe Brainard *(Coffee House Press), which came out late in 2004, and there is a great photo of the mag's teenage editorial board, reprinted from the May 27, 1959, issue of the* Tulsa Tribune. *Four clean-cut lads in Buddy Holly glasses preside over a paper-cluttered table. Gallup, Marsh, and Brainard smile at a more serious, contemplative Padgett as they "discuss the fine points of editing a 'little magazine,'" according to the caption.*

While I was working on this column, I became curious about Mountain, *the magazine David McFadden began publishing when he was 20. Turns out it's just about impossible to find the thing, but Paris, Ontario, bookseller (and world-class minimalist poet) Nelson Ball was willing to show me his personal copy of the first issue. It was similar to* The White Dove Review — *lively, mimeographed, precocious. Just as I see a parallel between the late gurus Ted Berrigan and bpNichol, there's a similar döppelganger effect between the wonder-filled personas of Padgett and McFadden.*

As for my stalking of Padgett, in November 2004, I flew to Chicago to catch him on his promotional tour for Joe *at the School of the Art Institute of Chicago. I mean, I was visiting my pal Richard Huttel too, and doing a reading with Richard, so it wasn't entirely suspicious. But before Padgett's reading (which was everything I could've hoped for), I dropped by the Art Institute itself, and near the end of my tour, saw a tall thin bald guy who I could've sworn was Padgett. We stared at each other as we passed. I wondered. We passed each other two or three more times, and I heard him speak with his companion; it was indeed Padgett. Later in the evening, I waited for the post-reading crowd around Padgett to subside, then I approached him. "Hi there, Ron," I said, extending a hand. "I'm Stuart Ross." Padgett quietly repeated my name, as his hand molecules touched mine, and then the light bulb went on above his head. "Security!" he called.*

HOW TO NOT WRITE

I REMEMBER WHEN poet Leona Gom came to do a reading in the common room of my high school, AISP, sometime around 1976. Kids could smoke in there. During the Q&A that followed, Gom mentioned that she hadn't written in a year and a half. Being a teenager who naturally wrote a dozen poems a day, all brilliant, I asked her how she could still call herself a poet. I don't remember her answer, but I was sure indignant.

Well, I haven't written a goddamn thing since January 1, when I wrote my annual New Year's poem. Even though it's been only a month and a half, I feel miserable. I wonder if I'm still a writer. I'm doing readings, and leading workshops, and bitching about other writers, so I'm displaying all the trappings of a writer. But I haven't had that satisfying feeling of *having written* for what seems like ages. I mean, I don't like the act of writing very much, but I do like having written.

Here is how I don't write: I lie on my side on my living room sofa and watch hours of CNN. I watch it less for information than to just observe the nature of its coverage. The CNN anchors don't piss me off as much as they did when they were blind, flag-waving parakeets last spring, during the Iraq invasion, but they still piss me off. Wolf Blitzer is so smug and self-satisfied, as is that weasel Aaron Brown. I liked it when Kim Novak got interviewed on *Larry King Live*, though. I once wrote a poem about her.

I run a bath and climb in and do the *Globe*'s Saturday cryptic cross-word. It's tricky to do in the bathtub without the newsprint getting soaked through. When I'm stumped, I toss the cryptic onto the floor and, from the heap of books on the back of the toilet tank, I select a collection of transcriptions of black-box recordings from airplane disasters. I add a little hot water to stretch my bath out another hour. An idea for a poem sidles into my brain and I make a mental note to remember it. Which I never do.

Towel wrapped around my waist, I track water into my living room again and check my email. I skim through all the messages from the Randy Newman listserv, and then the messages from the Editors' Association list, the Writers' Union list, Lexiconjury, and Smallpressers. I open an email from Lance in Wolfville. As usual, he's included a new poem. They're always good. I think about how I should write a poem. Instead, I get distracted by a spam headed "Break Through Walls With Your Cock."

I get dressed and drive my inherited, gas-guzzling 1989 Mercury Sable station wagon to a huge Goodwill in Etobicoke and spend a couple hours going through the books. Even though I already own more books than I can read before I die at 82, I buy 17 books, but I plan on selling eight of them on eBay. When I get home, I mix some grapefruit juice and cranberry juice, and settle in front of the TV and watch music videos. In the Britney vs. Christina thing, I'm in the Christina camp. I like that new Missy Elliott video where she does the King Kong schtick at the end. I also like that crazy video by that mock metal band, the Darkness, where a giant octopus engulfs the spaceship they're performing in. When Sarah McLachlan comes on, I change channels.

I started a novel last year, and by November I had 60 pages. It's got a lot of promise, but I just can't drag myself to the computer anymore to work on it. I could, however, pick up my little spiral-bound notebook and write a few poem titles. I often work like that — I write titles, then eventually I write poems under them. But I eat some potato chips instead. I'm putting on weight lately, and it makes me think of Ted Berrigan. I go and read some Berrigan lectures, because they inspire me for the poetry workshops I lead.

I phone Dana at work, but she's busy, so I phone Kevin. He reads me one of the nine poems he wrote the night before. I have a fleeting pang of resentment, but that quickly transforms to inspiration. I love his poems. After we hang up an hour later, having talked about Indian food, John Ashbery, our brothers, Eminem, Kev's cats' ailments, ECW Press: Good or Evil?, the Kennedy assassination, and pretzels, I take a half-step towards my poetry notebook. Then I whirl around, return to my computer, and spend the next two hours reading alternative news on InformationClearinghouse.info and CommonDreams.org, before checking out the latest numbers on IraqBodyCount.org.

Thinking about my novel again, I wander over to my bookshelves and start weeding to make room for the new books I bought. If I owned a Leona Gom book, I'd spare it.

March 2004

"ECW Press: Good or Evil?" That throwaway joke would become the final straw for some of the gang at ECW. Apparently I'd finally stepped over the line in the sand, though I didn't know it for a couple more months.

I'm still struggling with the novel.

JOHNNY STRIKES UP THE BAND

LIKE A LOT OF poets and other life forms, I like music. I like Bob Dylan and Roseanne Cash and Glenn Gould and Ernie K-Doe. I like the Original Five Blind Boys of Mississippi and Nick Lowe and Kristin Hersh and Al Jolson. I like John Cale a lot, and Ute Lemper and Melanie C. Also sublime are Ron Sexsmith and Dinah Washington. Tom Waits and Beth Orton sometimes make me cry, as does Roy Orbison. The Arrogant Worms and the Foremen make me laugh. Robert Wyatt fucks my brain up. The Clash is the best band ever.

In March, I drove three hours to check out Randy Newman performing with the Rochester Philharmonic Orchestra. My seat was excellent, third row centre, and it was exciting to watch Randy conduct the players through some of his movie music. I thought, Randy writes all these pop songs, but this is what he lives for: conducting an orchestra.

Over the past decade I've found myself reading to the accompaniment of various musicians, and I feel sort of how I think Randy felt. I'm not one of those poets who wants to be a rock star — I've never worn leather pants and I humbly report to the panel that I have no tattoos. What I do like is the opportunity to collaborate, and to be touched by the magic that is a person who can play music. Musicians are transcendent creatures. I'm in awe of them. I took eight years of piano, sight-reading like an ace, but I couldn't pick "Mary Had a Little Lamb" off a keyboard by ear if my life depended on it.

Recently, my old pal Mako Funasaka, who makes the TV series *Talkin' Blues* on Bravo!, invited me into a recording studio to jam with a couple of cool blues musicians, harpist David Rotundo and keyboardist Julian Fauth. The results were uneven (no fault of theirs; these guys are amazing), but we had a blast. I felt massively humbled in front of them, and they expressed admiration for us literary types. Also, they kept offering me swigs of Wild Turkey — at three o'clock in the afternoon! These guys know how to share.

A few months back, author, surrealism scholar, and reading series organizer Paul Bouissac threw me together with guitarist Shawn Rahbek and bassist David Almasy for a reading at Le Gourmand, a coffee shop just off Queen West. We met for the first time about 20 minutes before the hour-long performance. They had prepared a series of jazz standards, and I scrambled to match up my stories and poems with appropriate songs. We all had a great time, I was giddy, and everyone but Paul Dutton was very complimentary afterward.

In the fall, I was part of a Susan McMaster-curated Poetry Jam at the Ottawa International Writers Festival. Susan had insisted that I supply my texts weeks in advance, which left me disgruntled because I like spontaneity. But when I met with the half-dozen experimental jazz musicians — Geode Music & Poetry — minutes before showtime, they were game to throw all plans to the wind, and even try out an improvisational sound poem onstage. Again, the results were uneven, but there was a great sense of exploration, collaboration, camaraderie. We spent only 15 minutes onstage together, but I wanted to move in with them.

Another thing I like about this kind of performance is the new setting it can give to a piece of writing. Performing at the Furry Folk Festival the other week, I was onstage with a bunch of very cool folkies. I was about to read a short story unaccompanied and half-jokingly turned to keyboardist Tom Leighton, asking, "Got any cow music?" Leighton immediately broke into a loping shuffle, and I think a couple of guitarists joined in, too. I picked my way through "Cow Story," and it was like I was writing it while reading it.

The other thing about these musicians is they're all so damn friendly and respectful. They seem as happy for the opportunity as I am. Happy to cross over from one genre to another. Maybe somewhere in the depths of the music world, they're snipey cretins, just like poets, but I haven't seen it.

The first time I performed with musicians was back in the early 1990s. A few days before local band the Angry Shoppers were to appear on a godawful Rogers Cable TV show called *Amok*, their singer and their lead guitarist quit. Horn player Rick Bortolotti invited me to front the band (which included drummer Steve Lederman as well as a bassist and a sandwich maker), and in a few rushed practices, they adapted four of their tunes to my liveliest poems. I had to howl to be heard above these guys, and I maybe got a taste of the rock'n'roll thing. I jammed and performed with Steve and Rick a few more times, trying some pretty bizarre improvisational stuff, and we even gave ourselves a name: the Pod Squad (I'd told them about my nickname, Pods, given to me years earlier by Opal Nations). Then we went our separate ways. Our nonexistent fans were overcome with grief.

Oh, another musician I like is Warren Zevon. I hate that he is dead, but he sure made for the exit with class. I raise my Wild Turkey to you, Warren.

May 2004

A couple months later, Sandra Alland invited me to participate in her Language Lounge event at Mitzi's Sister on Queen West. She set up a blind date between me and experimental musician John Farrah. John and I had a few months to get together and work stuff out before our September gig, but we didn't get around to it till the day before (hey, it's just like writing university essays!), when I visited him at his studio above a great Portuguese bakery in our neighbourhood. He sat amidst his keyboards, and I plunked myself on a stool in the middle of the room, and we sipped tea. I noticed some Arabic writing framed on one of his walls, and he said he was Palestinian and I said I was Jewish, and we debated Middle East politics for an hour. Actually we didn't really debate; we agreed on everything, most notably our shared hatred of Bush, Rumsfeld, Cheney & Co. Our time was running out, so we attempted to get serious about our Language Lounge gig. After a half-hour of mutual sheepishness, a condition I was getting used to when meeting with musicians, we finally began to jam. We cracked each other up, and all went well. The next night, we took the stage and what John did musically bore almost no resemblance to what he'd done during the rehearsal, but somehow that made the experience all the sweeter.

Middle-aged Jewish pot-bellied surrealist poet seeks musicians for discreet improvisational encounters.

AT THE CONTROLS WITH
JOHNNY TURMOIL

THINGS ARE A TURMOIL! I rarely use the word *turmoil* — in fact, I may have never used it before, aloud or on paper — but my mother used it a lot. Great word.

My apartment is a mess, my car is dying, I've divorced my poetry publisher, my brother hasn't returned my phone messages since Passover (and since we're the entire family, that's a little alarming), I'm dragging my heels on an introduction to a poetry anthology that's coming out in the fall, I have 397 loose ends to tie up. But that is my perpetual state. Johnny Turmoil is my co-pilot.

And when I've got too much on my plate, I always go for another helping. So in the week before the spring Toronto Small Press Book Fair, with way too much already to do, I decided to publish a quickie chapbook of love poems for the U.S. president. I invited 50 writers from Canada, Europe, and the U.S., and most of them responded, almost instantly. I guess because we've all been feeling a lot of passion for Dubya lately. I got so excited putting together *My Lump in the Bed: Love Poems for George W. Bush* that I forgot I really didn't have the time to do it.

But amid the personal quagmire, I've written a bunch, so the self-loathing is subsiding just a little. I've made some serious inroads on a novel I've been hoping to write since my mother's death in 1995, a very cathartic novel, and I'm poking away at the occasional poem. I even created a one-minute puppet show called *The Ape Play* for 40 Tiny Queer Performances, an evening at Buddies in Bad Times curated by R.M. Vaughan. Man, I had fun with that — especially building the Ape House that sat on my knees for the show. I'm dreaming of doing a full-length version. I'm dreaming, in fact, of Broadway.

I feel a certain freedom, too, arising from the chaos. For the first time in ages, I have no idea who'll publish my next book of poems, should I manage to complete one. After four beautiful books, I've burned my bridges with ECW (the pivotal moment was a "We've had other priorities" response from the office when I politely inquired about an overdue freelance-editing invoice), and we're probably both relieved. It was a great relationship while it lasted. Some friends have suggested I move on to a bigger press, but I look forward to dealing with a way smaller house, one that doesn't put all its energy into celebrity biographies.

This month I turn 45, the speed of a single, so I have to accept that I'm an adult. Aside from the physical manifestations, little other evidence points in that direction. But one thing I've been able to accept finally is that I'm a writer. When people ask me what I do, I say, "I'm a writer." I don't say, "I make my living as an editor, but I also write." I don't say, "Oh, um, I write these, uh, weird little things sometimes." I don't say, "Hey, look at that big ant on the wall — behind you!" I write stories and poems, I teach workshops, I get published in magazines occasionally, I have some books out, I edit books by other writers. Why did it take me so long to be able to say, unquaveringly, "I'm a writer"? Some writers say they're a writer before they've published a word. Some of them say it when they're 20 years old. Let's kill those ones.

Maybe I had to feel like I'd written something good before I could say it. I think I wrote a really good poem just before Dana and I went to New York last month. I wanted to produce a poetry leaflet to leave around the city, but none of my poems seemed appropriate. So I decided to write a poem about New York, even though I'd never been there. I figured a poem about buildings would be a poem about New York, because apparently Manhattan was nothing but buildings, so I wrote a poem called "A Guy, Some Flippers, A Building."

You know that feeling you get when you write exactly the kind of poem you wanted to write? Maybe you get it more often than I do. I mean, I like a lot of my poems, but I don't think I'm anywhere close to where I'd like to be. This poem, though — "A Guy, Some Flippers, A Building" — it's a good poem. In fact, I'll put it up on my website, hunkamooga.com, so you can read it. If you get a second, tell me whether you think I'm a writer.

If I'm not, I'll keep trying. If I am, I don't have to worry about writing anything anymore. And that would be great, because it would give me some time to dig myself out of this never-ending turmoil.

July 2004

TOTAL STRANGERS! READING
MY BOOKS!

THERE ARE PEOPLE who know me who I don't know. I can't get used to that idea.

I was in Oakville recently, a wealthy little town west of Toronto, and dropped into Bookers. It's a pretty pleasant shop, balancing the fancy gift book with some good titles. They've got only a few dozen books in their poetry section, but I'll bet even that bit of shelf space doesn't pay for itself.

Anyway, I picked up a couple of books — a study of capital punishment by bestseller Scott Turow and *Kilter: 55 Fictions* by John Gould. As I left, I handed the very nice woman at the cash one of my poetry leaflets — "Civilization Sonnet" — and said she could read it if she had a free 14 seconds. She took the poem and said, "You're Stuart Ross?"

Out on the sidewalk, I began to roll it around in my noggin. Did she mean, "You're Stuart Ross, the guy whose name is on the cover of this leaflet?" or "You're Stuart Ross — I've heard of you"? Her tone suggested it was the latter, but since she was neither a friend of mine nor a relative, I know that's impossible.

But, look: a couple weeks back I did an outdoor reading to a small but appreciate audience at the Hillside Festival in Guelph, then wandered into a tent where Evalyn Parry was performing her amazing songs for a couple hundred people. I squeezed into a rare empty spot on a bench, and after a few minutes the woman to my right said, "Are you Stuart Ross?" She said I was her favourite at the Scream in High Park some summer past, and she mentioned one of my poems: "I think you read it at the Scream, or maybe I saw it on your website."

In my brain, I was going, *Oh my god, of all the people to sit beside in this tent, I've wound up beside a stalker.* And then my brain went, *Wait, she's just a person who saw me read once and she looked at my website. That's why I have a website — so people will look at it.* Then my brain went, *Good lord, are there people I don't know who look at my website?*

Further chilling evidence: at the Centauri Arts Retreat this past summer, where I was leading my Adventures in Poetry workshop, one of the participants mentioned that she had a couple of my books — she'd bought them even before she knew she was going to take my workshop.

"You mean, you bought them *before* you knew about Centauri?" I asked, stunned.

"Yeah," she said.

"And you've read them?"

"Oh yes."

"And you still decided to take this workshop?"

But enough about me. Let's talk about *Adventures in Poetry*. It's a landmark mimeographed magazine that New York poet Larry Fagin published between 1968 and 1975 — a dozen issues in total. I had one of them — and named my poetry workshop after it — but a few days ago a heap of them arrived in my mailbox from a used bookstore in Washington. I went fuckin' nuts! There's stuff in there by Ted Berrigan, Apollinaire, Anne Waldman, Siamese Banana Press publisher Johnny Stanton, Joe Brainard, Jim Dine, Bernadette Mayer, Aram Saroyan, Ron Padgett. It's endless, I tell you.

Fat, stapled mimeographed magazines full of experiment and adventure. There's nothing like it. It's all so much more visceral — so much more *heartfelt* — than the overpriced homogenous doorstoppers like *Descant* and *Exile* that pass for literary magazines today.

Now, through a convoluted series of connections, I had Larry Fagin's phone number, a number I never thought I'd call. But after revelling in all those *Adventures in Poetry*, I took a deep breath and picked up the phone. I've loved Fagin's poetry for many years, but I'm a guy who reads him who he doesn't know. I felt distinctly creepy dialling his number. And then he answered. I'm pretty awkward socially, especially when I'm in awe. I stammered out an introduction, then an apology, gushed about his mimeo past, and finally invited him to give me some poems for *Syd & Shirley*, the new poetry mag I'm working on. I was also curious about why he hadn't published a book of his poems since 1978's *I'll Be Seeing You* (Full Court Press), but didn't want to ask in case the answer was something really personal and maybe involved mental hospitals.

He sounded gruff and a little wary. No, he didn't have any poems for me. And he implored his students not to start up magazines. They're all terrible, he said, and no one reads the things. It would be far better if each of his students published just one chapbook of poetry a year. "I don't practice what I preach, though," he added, and he told me about his current magazine, *Sal Mimeo*. I laughed at the title and made a Gene Krupa reference (the actor Sal Mineo had played the jazz drummer in an old movie), and the conversation became easier. He was a great guy, after all.

Fifteen minutes later, I put down the phone. I'd just talked to Larry Fagin. What a weird concept. But I also knew that Larry Fagin would find it weird that I found it weird that I'd just talked to Larry Fagin.

There's a lesson in there somewhere. I think. (Now, don't you all go calling Larry Fagin!)

September 2004

A QUARTER-CENTURY OF BADLY
FOLDED LEAFLETS

I CAN'T HELP but wonder what impact a tiny literary press has on the world, or even on the local community. It's more important than an episode of the sitcom *Everybody Loves Raymond*, but less important than Nelson Mandela or Johnny Cash.

This year marks the 25th anniversary of Proper Tales Press, which I launched in 1979 so I'd have a poetry booklet to sell at a reading at the Axeltree Coffeehouse, a cozy, now-defunct venue in a church nestled in behind the Eaton Centre. Since then, I've put out heaps of chapbooks, leaflets, spiney books, litzines, postcards, and broadsides. After I published myself, I published friends like Kevin Connolly, Gary Barwin, Gil Adamson, Mark Laba, Lillian Necakov, and Michael Boyce, and also writers I had never met, like Vancouver's Wain Ewing and John M. Bennett from Columbus, Ohio. In 2003, I published a chapbook of poems by Elyse Friedman, whose only other book was a hardcover novel from Random House (nice to see someone using the big presses as a stepping stone to the small presses). Along the way, I've published a few of my literary heroes, too — Jim Smith, Opal Louis Nations, Joe Brainard, and, most recently, Bill Knott.

I've also cranked out a series of goofily titled mags: *Mondo Hunkamooga* (reviewing the small press), *Who Torched Rancho Diablo?* (poetry and fiction), *Dwarf Puppets on Parade* (poetry and fiction with prescribed restrictions), and *Peter O'Toole* (one-line poems). Some of them lasted many years, while others only an issue or two. My next mag is *Syd & Shirley*, named after my late parents. Each issue will contain about a dozen poems by each of three or four poets (both Canadian and American), plus an interview and capsule book reviews. I hope to make it a going concern.

The Proper Tales Press publications are often important to the writers I publish — in some cases, they've marked an author's first time in print. And because I've also used Tales as an ongoing self-publishing project, it's had an enormous impact on me, and perhaps on how I write. But why do I do it? (And I've been running a tiny literary press longer than anyone I know, with the exception of jwcurry, who started the same year.) Why do I fold and staple while the other children are out playing? I've thought a few times about giving up Proper Tales and concentrating on my own writing — I could have written so much more without Tales — but in the end it's like breathing. Gotta keep doing it. Here I am, still not finished my first full-length novel at age 45, while all these young pups around me are writing up a storm and winning Pulitzer Prizes and getting zillion-dollar advances. I mean, 12-year-old novelists are buying houses in Rosedale. But I made the decision to be a publisher and I'm stuck with it, probably till I croak.

There are others like me — Daniel f. Bradley, Marshall Hyrciuk, Carleton Wilson, Jay MillAr, Derek Beaulieu, Karen Sohne, and tons more — who both write themselves and publish the works of others through micropresses. And then there's Bev Daurio and Alana Wilcox, both fine writers and the best editors I know, who have taken on major literary presses (Mercury and Coach House, respectively) and must struggle to find a tiny pocket of space to do their own writing. They probably question themselves about it every day. Brian Kaufman of Vancouver's Anvil Press is in the same boat, and Beth Follett of Pedlar Press, and didn't Gary Geddes start up Cormorant Press? Hell, even the inscrutable Jack David wrote the occasional poem before he and Robert Lecker started up ECW in 1742.

And then there are writers who put everything into their own work. They don't have their own presses and they don't promote the work of others. It wouldn't even occur to them. Or they have their own press, but they publish only themselves. I remember indie guru and *Broken Pencil* founder Hal Niedzviecki once badgering one such writer — that she had a responsibility to contribute to the community! — but while I half-agree, I'd say that the writing is contribution enough.

The other night, as I folded 200 copies of the leaflet "Three Arms Less," a short story of mine, I wondered how many sheets of paper I've folded in my life. And how many sheets of cover stock I've scored, and how many staples I've pounded into a saddle-stitched booklet. It's sorta scary. I could've spent all that time watching *Everybody Loves Raymond*.

What have I accomplished with Proper Tales Press? I've published about 60 books and perhaps 75 leaflets; about a dozen postcards, 10 broadsides, and a sound-poetry audiocassette. (An almost complete list is on my website, hunkamooga.com.) I've made a lot of friends, provided some entertainment, lost thousands of dollars, earned some readers, helped expose work I believed in, gave shape to my writing career. Some of the books sold out; some were dismal distribution failures. I still have lots of copies of Randall Brock's 1982 minimalist-poetry collection *Shadows of Seclusion*. It's a damn good book. Brock, a loner poet from Spokane, Washington, phoned me almost weekly until the mid-'80s: "Stu," he'd drawl, "how many copies of *Shadows* left?" And years after I published Jim Smith's masterful *Convincing Americans*, I dumped a couple boxes of them on his porch and fled.

November 2004

I, THE NEW ROD McKUEN!

WHY MUST POETRY be this miserable, bleak, negative, depressing thing that I've been propagating for close to 30 years? Why evoke the blahs when I can bring joy and hope to the shivering masses?

I think of poor, sweet Winifred Ely, the supervisor of the teenage page team at Bathurst Heights Library back in the 1970s. I was a page then, and a freak: a 15-year-old with a big tangled afro and a cluster of tikis hanging around my neck. Books by Kids had recently published *The Thing in Exile*, a small collection of poems by me and my friends Steve Feldman and Mark Laba. Steve was the cute one, the sort of Davy Jones of the trio, and he wrote poems of love and emotion. Mark and I wrote poems about insects, reptiles, alienation, death, and dismemberment. Well, a few days after my library received the book, Win stopped me on my way out the staff door at closing time.

"I read your poems," she said with a compassionate smile, a warm hand on my shoulder. "Are you OK?"

"Sure," I said, forcing a smile, my tikis clacking against my chest. Did she really think that because I wrote this depressing shit I was a miserable kid? I mean, I sort of was, but still . . .

Anyway, here's the thing: for the past bunch of years, I've been writing a poem on New Year's Day and sending it to the several hundred friends, colleagues, and acquaintances who comprise my email list. This year, on the morning of January 1, what weighed on me was the death toll and survivor misery of the Asian tsunami, and, on a more personal level, that another year had passed and my parents and brother Owen were still dead. In fact, 2005 would be the 10th anniversary of my mother's last breath, a breath I witnessed. I sat back in bed with my laptop and I wrote a poem about the tsunami dead and my family dead. I had to write that poem. But there was no way I could send it out to everybody and bum them on this New Year's Day. On the other hand, really, how was it possible to think of anything else on that day? The death toll from the tsunami was creeping up above 120,000. Should I write a poem about kittens and lollipops?

Late in the afternoon, I pored through the pages of poets whose work I loved: Dick Gallup, Bill Knott, David McFadden, Ron Padgett, Dean Young, Campbell McGrath, Lisa Jarnot, Joe Brainard, Elaine Equi, Nelson Ball. I did everything I could to trigger a new poem, something that might hover above the abyss, something I could send out that day. Again, I began typing, and what emerged was a seven-part poem that was downright weird, even by my standards. Now, I don't usually think about audience when I write, but the New Year's poem is supposed to be a sort of gift to those I know. I was so goddamn self-conscious. I couldn't inflict this burst of nutso verse on them either.

I ordered some Chinese food, watched a couple of movies, checked out some godawful videos on MuchMusic (I'm elderly now and cannot take seriously the three-chord angst of 20-year-olds), read some more

96

poets. It was after 10 in the evening. I had two hours to write my poem and send it out. For my friends in Scotland, England, and the Netherlands, it was already too late, already tomorrow.

Something clicked: "Dear pant legs, / I slip my legs / into you," I wrote. "Dear necktie, / I tie you around my neck. / Dear shirt, you hide / my considerable belly, / you warm my freckled arms." I knew I was on a roll, but had no idea where it was all going to end up. But I could kill time with socks, like when you add fingers onto your stick figure in a game of hangman. "Dear socks, how is / the weather around my feet, / around each separate toe? / Dear door, I slip through / the wood of you / quietly. Dear street, / dusted with snow, you / cradle my car and —" And what? Holy shit! The clock was ticking! " — pass it along to the grocery store." Yeah! The grocery store! Christ, I'm a genius!

This was it, though: the end was near. Somehow, I had to rustle up some kernel of optimism. It was either that or send out the goddamn tsunami poem. I started tapping again: "Dear unwobbling display / of canned niblets, you nourish me / that I might prepare / for the days ahead, / the days with a new name, / and the people that people them . . ." Could I do it? It went against my grain, but I had to deliver the gift: " . . .the wonderful things they contain."

Jesus Christ, was I a fraud? Did I believe this? Did I believe there'd be "wonderful things"? Well, I did hope against hope. I sent the thing out. Though it was already near midnight, responses began to trickle in almost immediately and continued through the next day: "well filled and well feeled," "spirited and humorous," "touching," "beautiful," "oh bliss bliss," "what a lovely way to look at the days to come," "Are you expecting?" and this one: "thanks for making me smile, and for making me hope." Shit, I had actually made people *happy* with my poem! It was the new me, the 2005 me: Poet of Joy, Optimism, and Good Times.

And what of Steven Feldman? Steve's had a very rough couple of decades, waltzing with the psychiatric universe, battling demons in his head and in white coats. He's never stopped writing, but *his* writing has gotten a lot darker. A few months back, he released a book of his poems (*In the Shallow Noise*) and an accompanying CD of his songs (*Living in a Picture Show*). It's a bumpy ride, not unlike Steve's adult life, but there's a lot that's brilliant in the package. Some of it's downright harrowing. Grab a copy in better Toronto bookstores and CD shops, or email sleepingsoundpublishing@sympatico.ca for info on how to get a copy.

Gotta run now. I've got poems about kittens to write — *dead* kittens.

February 2005

GIVE PAGE A CHANCE

IF WE WERE all struck mute, where would poetry be? Well, on the page, I guess, where it belongs. A strange thing for me to say, perhaps, because doing readings is my favourite part of being a writer.

But readings can be counterproductive. I think of the show-biz atmosphere of Toronto's Lexiconjury, run by Bill Kennedy and Angela Rawlings, and Vancouver's Thundering Word Heard, run by T-Paul Ste. Marie. I've appeared in both series, and it was a blast in both cases, with enthusiastic audiences and hosts, but somehow the series themselves seemed more important than the readers. As if the readers were there to fill up the spaces necessary to make the series happen instead of the series existing to give the poets a soapbox. Suddenly poetry is as much about performance and personality as it is about the writing. Hell, even looks play a part (though I still manage to get a good response).

Reading series like the Lex and TWH, as well as Ottawa's Tree, Toronto's Suburban Spoken Word, Hamilton's LitLive, and Victoria's Mocambopo, are also very much about scene-making. Perhaps another word, and a more positive one, would be *community*. They are social events, and sometimes the actual readings can seem like the evil excuse necessary for a bunch of writers to get together, drink beer, and talk. I mean, there's usually more break time than there is reading time. That's not a bad thing, of course. Writing is a solitary job, and we need to talk with others like us. And for those just starting out in this mug's game, readings provide a venue for learning, for meeting mentors, for confirming that one is not alone and all is not (completely, anyway) futile. But the average reading-goer spends more money on beer at readings than on poetry books. Says something about priorities.

The most important thing a reading can do is make an audience member aware of a writer she's never heard of before. For me, as a writer, it's also motivation to get some new shit together, an opportunity to test-drive pieces that I haven't read before. On another, less noble level, it's a chance to get a bit of adulation or response in an art practice that doesn't offer much of anything else as recompense. But for me, the greatest pay-off in writing poetry is the personal satisfaction it delivers. Creating something I'd actually like to read myself.

This emphasis on public readings distracts from the art. It encourages poetry that panders to the audience. It emphasizes performance over good lines and images. You see that especially in open mics and spoken word events. You want to pick up a chair and hurl it at the reader's head, just to defend the honour of poetry, even though poetry usually doesn't deserve it.

What is important about poetry is all those words that make up the poem, and nothing else. Look at the way the words lie on the field of a page. A poem by Nelson Ball does indeed look like bird tracks on hard snow (the title of one of his books): there is far more empty page than printed page, suggesting that much has been left unsaid, or, alternatively, that what needs to be said is simple and modest. On the page, Nelson's poems are quiet and intelligent, like Nelson himself. A poem by John Barlow will often crowd the page, bumping at the margins, straining for a bigger field to fit into. There's so much to say and it goes all over the place. A single page of John's dense poetry is a metaphor for his entire work: there's sloppy heaps of it, and the art is the accumulation.

Without seeing either of these guys onstage, just examining how their words deal with the rectangular white operating table that is the page, we get a sense of who they are. And Nelson Ball doesn't do readings, anyway. I've been to three Nelson Ball readings, all of them book launches: at one, I read Nelson's poems (he'd sneakily auditioned me over the phone without my knowing it); at another, Richard Truhlar read his poems; and at the best Ball reading, Victor Coleman had Nelson's poems beamed by overhead projector onto a screen, where they lingered for maybe 30 seconds each. The packed rear room of the Rivoli was silent, as Nelson, tucked into a back corner watching along, "read" a couple dozen of his poems without uttering a word.

John Barlow's readings are excruciating, frustrating, mesmerizing. He flips open his books, or shuffles through his loose pages, bewildered and yet fascinated by himself, begins reading a piece, then decides he's had enough, often in mid-line, and jumps to another. It's hard to tell what's poem and what's preamble, interamble, or postamble. Each piece blends into the next, punctuated by John's nervous giggle and existential groans. At a launch at Top of the Senator for one of his Exile books, he read the table of contents as if they were a poem; at a reading at the University of Toronto, he rifled through his manuscript pages for several minutes, sighing, giggling, moaning, stammering, then left the podium without having read a single word.

For Ottawa's Michael Dennis, who's been doing readings for nearly 30 years, though with decreasing frequency (since he demands, on principle, $200 to show up), the poems themselves really are the thing. Michael reads more poetry than anyone I know, and when he reads his own poems, you can tell he loves poetry. A natural raconteur and consummately swell guy, he's totally comfortable with an audience. On the opening night of the Ottawa International Writers Festival a few years back, on a bill with Pierre Berton and Pierre Berton's bow tie, Michael stole the show. It wasn't ego that did it, or a rock'n'roll performance (though he did get the audience la-la-ing the *Hockey Night in Canada* theme) — he just seemed to want to make those who filled the seats in the National Arts Centre love poetry as much as he did.

On the other end of the spectrum, Toronto poet and micropresser Daniel f. Bradley is so uncomfortable reading publicly that he once read with his back to the audience. To the flesh audience, that is — he was facing a cut-out paper audience he'd constructed and propped against the wall in front of him. At another memorable appearance, at Clint Burnham's Stoopid Reading Series in Kensington Market, Daniel read only his failed grant applications. He seemed more comfortable with that.

(I've blithered on only about poetry readings here; fiction is a whole other ball game. Maybe because fiction is longer: it's more like symphony than rock'n'roll. Maybe because there's no way to hide dreadful, work-manlike prose with bells and whistles. A Jim Munroe reading proves that. One of my favourite readers of fiction is Hull's John Lavery, who has two bizarre, spectacular story collections out from ECW Press. In conversation, John is almost painfully quiet, his voice falling just below the ambient noise of the room. In front of an audience he's pure vaudeville, but his possessed readings only emphasize the pure mastery of his sentences. Scotland's A.L. Kennedy is an astonishing reader of her work: she's gut-punchingly funny when she means to be funny, and she's always understated and brooding. You know you are staring into the dangerous maw of great literature when she reads. Same with Gil Adamson, a Toronto writer who is terrified of doing readings. You can't tell she's terrified: she just reads, seemingly calmly, and knocks you flat with the freshness of her words.)

My friend Eddy Yanofsky, a fine and modest poet who for years ran the University of Toronto Bookstore Reading Series, back when it was actually good, bristles when the writers at a reading are called *readers*. He turned to me once at the Art Bar and said, "Why do they say, 'Tonight's readers are . . .' instead of 'Tonight's writers are . . .'?" Maybe it's time to reclaim the word *reader* for the person who reads the poem on the page instead of the *writer* who's standing at a mic.

So let's talk about poetry on the page for another minute. In his essay "Live Yak Pie," James Tate, the Pulitzer Prize-winning American poet whose *Shroud of the Gnome* should be at the top of your must-read list, writes:

> *When you come upon a poem you especially like, what separates it from so many other well-made poems is the quality of its insight. And for this word* insight *I would happily substitute the loftier words* revelation *or* epiphany. . . .
>
> *The act of writing poetry is a search for the unknown. Each line written is searching for the next line. And as the weight, the length, of the poem accumulates, so too does the pressure accumulate for a revelation to occur. Each image or idea should point the way to another image or idea. And each of these indicates the need for further development if the poem is to achieve its maximum potential. Each poem dictates the magnitude of the revelation. An extremely small insight can be satisfying. Simply offering the reader a new way of seeing a common object or familiar experience qualifies as an insight or epiphany.*

Maybe sitting in a bar surrounded by others who are scrawling poems on napkins in preparation for the open mic (or the "open michelle," as it's annoyingly called at Lexiconjury; as if there's something sexist about "mic") isn't the best place to drink in tiny epiphanies. It's a very personal thing, your relation to a poem you love. And from the poem's point of view, too, it's better if there's no audience around, no amplified sound, no cappuccino machine.

A good poem is an alien looking for an earthling host. It doesn't want anyone watching when it drills its metallic tentacle into your skull and lays its egg inside your blobby brain.

YOU ALWAYS KILL THE ONE YOU LOVE . . . WRITING WITH

MURDER AND COLLABORATION go hand-in-hand. Because to create art with someone else is to eventually want to throttle them and leave them in a ditch on a rural road near Kleinberg, where they'll be discovered by a lost snowmobiler at the tail end of winter. But there are other good things that come out of the collaborative process, too!

Collaboration is a natural part of other arts — music, theatre, film, dance — but is rare in literature. A few of my favourite collaborative works: James Tate and Bill Knott's demented novel *Lucky Darryl* (Release Press, 1977); Ron Padgett and Joe Brainard's text-with-graphics *100,000 Fleeing Hilda* (Boke Press, 1967); *Double Down: Reflections on Gambling and Loss* (Houghton Mifflin, 1999), brothers Steven and Frederick Barthelme's beautiful memoir of gambling addiction; Tom Veitch and Ron Padgett's (yes, demented) novel *Antlers in the Treetops* (Coach House Press, 1973); *In England Now That Spring* (Aya Press, 1979), visual and poetic collabs by Steve McCaffery and bpNichol, who also worked together as the Toronto Research Group; Tom Clark and Ted Berrigan's (well . . . demented) satire *Bolinas Eyewash* (unpublished, 1971; pirate editions exist); and John Ashbery and James Schuyler's nearly unreadable but somehow still delightful novel *A Nest of Ninnies* (Z Press, 1975). One of these days I'll have the courage to crack open the novel *Piccolo Mondo* (Coach House Books, 1998), by the quartet of George Bowering, Angela Bowering, Michael Matthews, and David Bromige.

I've collaborated on poems, sound poems, short stories, and novellas, and while it's always been a maddening experience ending in clumsy Patricia Highsmith-inspired homicide, it's also been artistically enriching. There are a few particularly cool things about collaborating.

First, it forces you to write, because your collaborator is breathing down your neck, and also because you're given something to react to: a line of poetry, a paragraph of prose, a plot twist. I've often collaborated when I just haven't been able to write on my own.

Second, it lets you do things you wouldn't normally do. That's partly because you're relieved of full responsibility in a collaboration, so you feel freer to experiment. Also, you and your collaborator naturally move towards each other's styles so that the resultant text will have a unified voice. Or maybe you both go off together into a completely new realm.

Third, when some asshole criticizes a line or paragraph in your collaboration, you can say, "I didn't write that part."

My first collaborator was Mark Laba. Mark and I grew up on the same Bathurst Manor street in suburban Toronto in the early 1960s. At age four, we were best friends. We filled up a little red wagon with sand and roamed the streets with our mobile insect cemetery. Then, in high school, we began working on two-voice sound poems, which we performed all over the place for about a decade. Our joint work in poetry culminated in an hour-long performance at the Toronto Mini-Festival of Sound

Poetry in 1988, where bpNichol, who hosted the evening, declared Mark the "Louis Armstrong of sound poetry." I think it had something to do with the volume of sweat he produced. A cassette of this performance, called *Preacher Explodes During Sermon*, was jointly released in 1988 by Underwhich Editions and Proper Tales Press. Laba didn't show up for the launch, so I had to kill him.

Mark and I also wrote a serialized pork noir novel called *The Pig Sleeps*, published over six installments in *What!* magazine during the 1980s and later released in its entirety by Katy Chan's Contra Mundo Books. We worked closely on the project, discussing each twist in the plot. Mark specialized in over-the-top hard-boiled similes, while I looked after much of the dialogue. Looking at the thing, I can no longer remember who wrote what. Mark and I had known each other for so long that we fused our styles together effortlessly.

And back in 1985, my high school pal David Fine and I wrote our only collaboration: a surreal, grotesque short story called "The Esther Rhine Shrine Memorial Clock," which I published as a leaflet through jwcurry's 1cent series. David, along with his wife, Alison Snowden, later won an Oscar for Best Animated Short and created the cartoon TV series *Bob and Margaret*. From fiction leaflet to TV series: how the mighty have fallen.

But my other major collaborator was the writer and musician Gary Barwin, who I'd met at York University. In the early '90s we created some sound poems together, primarily to present at a couple of performance-art festivals in Cleveland, Ohio, again culminating in a live cassette, *These Are the Clams That I'm Breathing, These Are the Clams That I'm Breathing* (Burning Press, 1992). We also wrote a few poems for the page, and a couple of short stories that never saw publication. And once I stayed at Gary's house in Hamilton for a week while we collaborated on an insane short novel, *The Mud Game* (The Mercury Press, 1995). The process was different this time, one we'd honed in our Cleveland motel room. One of us would sit at the keyboard, writing as much or as little as we pleased, and then the other would take over. We didn't discuss the plot; we just tried to kill off each other's characters and make things miserable for one another. It was an interesting collaboration: I don't think Gary and I tried much to meld our styles: instead we sparred. I'd written a lot more fiction than Gary at the time, so I think it was more of a stretch for him than for me. I'm happy as a clam with the results, though, and we had a blast doing readings from the novel. Too bad I had to kill Gary.

Jim Smith and I gave a pathetic stab at a collaborative novel around the same time, planning to alternate chapters. We did one chapter each of what was to be called *Freezing the Geeks*, or perhaps *Freezing Out the Geeks*, and then we gave up. I'll always regret that. I still have those two chapters kicking around in a box somewhere: it was going to be a radical, political sci-fi novel. Everything Jim wrote was radical and political. I think it might have worked had we adapted the Barwin/Ross/Laba method of writing while in the same room together. On the bright side, because we never finished, no one had to die, though Jim did give up writing to become a lawyer. I believe the French call that the "tiny death."

SOMETIMES I FEEL LIKE A CHILDLESS WRITER, OR REGRETS, I'VE HAD, UH, TWO

TODAY'S TOPIC IS regret. Here are two such tales.

I didn't think I was ever going to get to New York, because I was scared of New York. Not scared of getting mugged, or having buildings fall on me, but scared of the sheer size of the city. I mean, Chicago overwhelmed me the first time I went there — just seemed so big and old and sprawling. So there was no way I was going to survive New York. Also, I never have any idea what direction I'm walking in. If I go into a phone booth, I'm lost by the time I come out. So how would I survive la Manzana Grande?

It was stupid. There I am, practically taking baths in New York poetry — bubble baths! — and I couldn't muster up the courage to visit the site of all those Frank O'Hara poems. But I did get to New York finally, at age 44, in May 2004. Dana, my girlfriend, is way braver than I am, and her dad took her family there every year when she was a kid, so she was fearless about it.

Anyway, we walked the streets that had been walked by O'Hara, John Ashbery, Ted Berrigan, Joe Brainard, Kenward Elmslie, Ron Padgett, Kenneth Koch, Larry Fagin, James Schuyler, Dick Gallup, and, oh, lots of other people (Parker Posey, Patricia Highsmith, and John Cheever come to mind, but I'm sticking to poets, OK?). I wandered into St. Mark's Church, home of the legendary Poetry Project, and a dashing British guy predictably named Miles Champion gave me a warm welcome when I told him I was a Canadian pilgrim. I bought some stuff, he gave me some stuff, I tried to do some surreptitious snooping, we chatted a bit. Actually, I'd been too shy to go into the Poetry Project's cluttered little office, but Dana dragged me in, knowing I'd be tortured by regret if I didn't do it.

I left the church, my knees weak. Took the requisite photos. That afternoon, I walked by Ron Padgett's apartment building in the Village and imagined him trying to open the front door, his arms filled with groceries, a woodpecker peering at him from a nearby tree. Woody Woodpecker, in fact. Somewhere in this city, John Ashbery was still around, getting real old, perhaps writing his follow-up to *Chinese Whispers*. Kenward Elmslie was maybe eating leftover cake from his 75th birthday party and thinking of Joe. Somewhere there was a garbage dump or landfill cradling the empty bottles of Pepsi that Ted Berrigan had inhaled.

So I go back to the writing of all these poets, and I feel like I've gotten a little closer to the work. I've been to some of the places I read about, I've smelled the air, I've weaved my way through the crowded sidewalks. New York is no longer a movie to me, and it's no longer as distant as other places I've never been to, like Paris, Jerusalem, New Delhi, and Berlin.

About New York, I've averted regret.

*   *   *

I have some long-time friends who think that I write a lot. They, too, wanted to write, but instead wound up raising families. Once their children have grown up and left home, these friends plan to write the books that have been building up in them all these years.

I have strong regrets about not having kids. These days I feel like I'd trade all my books for a normal life. In this normal life, I have a unionized job, perhaps in a library, and my partner works, too, and we have a couple of kids. I get a lot of reading done, and wonder what life would be like had I opted out of the normal and dedicated myself to writing. Maybe I wish I'd become a writer instead of changing diapers and dreading my kids' teen years.

This either/or thing, though — I know it's a ruse. It's just an excuse for my cowardice. I could have written books *and* raised some kids. I know lots of people who've done that. My writer friends Lance La Rocque, Elyse Friedman, Brian Panhuyzen, Mark Laba, and Clint Burnham have all become parents over the past few years. Gary Barwin had a couple dozen of them years ago, and Daniel Bradley is about to have one. I'm certainly no more unlikely a parent than they are. I'm in awe of them, humbled by their courage and commitment. It's harder for them, but they find time to write. I feel like a lazyass in comparison.

So I never had kids, likely never will have that experience of looking at a kid who is my kid, and my older brothers never had kids. At 45, I just don't feel settled enough to be a father. I can barely keep up with my own dishes. It tears me apart that my parents had wanted grandkids so badly, and all they got — from me, at least — was absurd stories and surreal poems. So that's it for this branch of the Rosses. It all stops with me. Instead of a kid surviving me, I'll have a bunch of weird books. (Well, my kid might have been weird, too.) When my friend Tom Walmsley thought he was going to die within a year or so, because the chances of his getting a new liver were becoming pretty slim, he wrote like a fiend. That was it — he'd go down writing. A novel trilogy, a poetry sequence, a screenplay, a stage play or two. He didn't finish all of those before his deadline was up, but he did get a new liver.

I think I'm writing for a similar reason. And I've noticed that I write increasingly about my family. As if I can keep my family going through my writing. In fact, I named my new poetry magazine, *Syd & Shirley*, after my parents, because I want them to somehow be involved in my writing, and I want their names to be stuck together, as if they're still a bridge team, ready to take on Anne and Stan, or Bill and Belle.

I creep in wearing my pyjamas while they're shuffling the cards, and I steal a few peanuts out of one bowl, and a few ju-jubes out of another. My dad catches me and puts me in a headlock.

RETURN TO PLATEN PLACE

I PUNCH MY little fingers onto the different letter discs that top the keys, and the metal hammers fling upward towards the rubber roller. A black ribbon leaps up to soften the blow, insinuating itself between hammer and roller. Sometimes the hammers reach the roller, and sometimes they don't. If they do, they leave a glistening mark against the black rubber. I bend forward and squint at the mark. It is a letter. Or maybe a question mark. Or some other mark I don't know the name of.

I like the sound the keys make when I strike them, and I like the little clack the hammer makes when it hits the roller through the ribbon. I like the glistening marks the procedure produces on the roller, and I lightly glide my fingertips along the hard rubber surface. It gives in only the most imperceptible way, but still it feels smooth and cool, very pleasing. My fingertips become a purplish black, which eventually ends up on my face and my bare legs, and my T-shirt, and on the wall. When I get called to lunch, it ends up on the spongy white bread of my grilled-cheese sandwich.

Thus I become a writer.

It's not long before I learn to slip a sheet of paper into the Underwood manual typewriter, and roll it into position with the knob on the end of the carriage, making that pleasing *clickedy-clickedy* noise. I punch at the keys again and letters appear on the paper, and words eventually, and I learn to slap the silver lever at the left of the carriage to advance the paper to the next line.

If I don't punch the key hard enough, the hammer doesn't completely reach the paper, and I get only a faint image of the letter, or nothing at all. I might need to hit the backspace key, tugging the carriage backward a notch, and retype the fudged letter. Soon I can type without getting ink on my grilled-cheese sandwich.

The Underwood isn't much different from the typewriter the artist Rodney Graham employs in his installation piece "Rheinmetall/Victoria 8." It's a few decades later that I sit on the cold concrete floor of 303 Gallery in New York City's Chelsea district, and stare at the far wall. Directly to my left in the cool, cavernous room is a Victoria 8, a massive Italian 1950s projection machine through which film threads along a nearly slapstick looped route. On the wall, projected large, a 1930s manual German typewriter, the Rheinmetall, is gradually covered in powdery snow, its stark black keys eventually cupping pleasing little white mounds, its platen and carriage disappearing beneath snowdrifts.

In 1980, I'm sitting in front of a Brother electric typewriter in Charlie Huisken's Queen Street East bookstore, This Ain't the Rosedale Library, one of the great literary landmarks of my writing life. (The store still exists, on Church Street, in the heart of Toronto's gay ghetto, and Charlie's still there, the always-curious, idealistic indie bookseller, along with his business partner, the painter Dan Bazuin.) It's the weekend of the third International Three-Day Novel-Writing Contest, run by Vancouver's Pulp Press, and I'm one of three novelists-in-residence in the store, flanked by Paul Quarrington and Burke Campbell. I've just come up with the ending to *Wooden Rooster*, a picaresque tale of a Latin American carpenter named Carlos Venom whose life has gone horribly wrong. I send him to the Arctic, where he is allowed the reprieve of frolicking among Christ-like penguins before meeting the fate of the Rheinmetall. I feed sheet after sheet of three-hole-punched white paper into my electric Brother. Each time I get to the end of a line, the carriage returns automatically. Technology has come so far.

Not long after that, at York University, I become the typesetter for the student newspaper *Excalibur*. I sit behind the humongous, L-shaped A&M Varityper CompEdit 5900, keying in stupid articles about college sports. One of the football team's players is named Ross MacDonald; I type in parentheses next to his name "no relation to the creator of hard-boiled detective Lew Archer," just because I have the power to do that. After all, I am The Typesetter, and I sit behind this mystical machine that only I can operate. No one will argue with me. As I tap the keys at 70 words per minute (I've slowed down considerably since), a small font wheel in the CompEdit's bowels spins at lightning speed; when the required letter is lined up with the lens, a flash of light exposes its shape onto photographic paper. I love the grinding *clank* when I change fonts and the font wheel carousel revolves, or when I instruct the machine to increase the type size and the lens carriage moves accordingly. When I'm finished an article, I command the photographic paper to advance into a large metal cassette, pull a blade across to cut the paper, and haul the cassette into the darkroom and put it through the processor, then hang up the length of paper with clothespins to dry. At night, when the newspaper's done, I stick around and typeset *Wooden Rooster*. It didn't win the Three-Day Novel-Writing Contest, so I'm publishing it myself through my Proper Tales Press imprint.

Good lord, I'm only 45 and I've lived through all these technologies.

As I type this, one blizzardy afternoon in January 2005, I'm lying propped up in bed, my knees drawn up, my fingers plucking away at an iBook wedged against belly and thigh. No ink has been harmed in the writing of this column, no grilled-cheese sandwiches blemished.

ANSWERS TO "HOW'S YER SMALL PRESS BRAINS?" (PAGE 61)

1. Opal Louis Nations.

2. *Mountain.*

3. Correct answers include: 1cent, Curvd H&z, *Industrial Sabotage*, Spider Plots in Rat Holes, Utopic Furnace, Room 3o2 Books, *Spudburn.*

4. 1987, at the Hart House Pub on University of Toronto campus.

5. Correct answers include: John Ashbery, Bill Berkson, Ted Berrigan, Joe Brainard, Kenward Elmslie, Larry Fagin, Dick Gallup, Barbara Guest, Kenneth Koch, David Lehman, Eileen Myles, Frank O'Hara, Ron Padgett, James Schuyler, Lewis Warsh.

6. Four Horsemen (Dutton). Owen Sound (Dean).

7. Lowlife Publishing, run by Maggie Helwig.

8. The walnut.

9. Nelson Ball and Barbara Caruso.

10. *Mondo Hunkamooga, Who Torched Rancho Diablo?, Dwarf Puppets on Parade, Peter O'Toole.*

11. Black Moss Press, Virgo Press, Coach House Press.

12. *Essays on Canadian Writing.*

13. blewointmentpress (Nightwood). Aya Press (Mercury).

14. Correct answers include: Gil Adamson, Tony Burgess, Victor Coleman, Kevin Connolly, Lynn Crosbie, Connie Deanovich, Brian Dedora, David Demchuk, Greg Evason, Gail Harris, Daniel Jones, Lillian Necakov, Stuart Ross, Randall Schroth.

15. Photocopying.

16. Alana Wilcox. *A Grammar of Endings.*
17. James Tate. *Lucky Darryl.*
18. The News.
19. Joe Rosenblatt.
20. Hermann Neutics.
21. *Tish* (1960s). *The Shit* (1980s).
22. *Class Warfare.*
23. Dennis Cooper.
24. Streetcar Editions. His asshole.
25. *Double Persephone*, published by Hawkshead Press.

INDEX

ABOUT THE AUTHOR

Stuart Ross is a prolific writer, publisher, editor, and teacher. He has been active in the underground literary scene for over 25 years. He's sold 7,000 copies of his poetry and fiction chapbooks in the mean streets, co-founded the Toronto Small Press Book Fair, trained insurgents in his Poetry Boot Camps, and given readings across Canada and abroad. Stuart has edited several literary magazines, most recently *Syd & Shirley*, as well as the anthology *Surreal Estate: 13 Canadian Poets Under the Influence*. His column "Hunkamooga" appears in *Word: Toronto's Literary Calendar*. Stuart's 2003 collection, *Hey, Crumbling Balcony! Poems New & Selected*, was published to critical acclaim and sporadic irritation. His online home is hunkamooga.com.